How To...
Read Music

By Mark Phillips

ISBN 978-1-4950-0146-8

HAL•LEONARD®
CORPORATION
7777 W. BLUEMOUND RD. P.O. BOX 13819 MILWAUKEE, WI 53213

In Australia Contact:
Hal Leonard Australia Pty. Ltd.
4 Lentara Court
Cheltenham, Victoria, 3192 Australia
Email: ausadmin@halleonard.com.au

Visit Hal Leonard Online at
www.halleonard.com

CONTENTS

CHAPTER 1

BEFORE YOU START

WHAT IS MUSIC READING?

When you read music, you decipher information conveyed by symbols called *notes* that appear on a five-line grid called a *staff*. Then you use that information to play the music on your instrument, or just to hear it in your mind if you're a super-advanced musician like Bach or Mozart!

This is what *notes* look like. Notice that they come in various shapes:

This is what a *staff* looks like:

SOME REAL MUSIC

This is what notes look like on a staff:

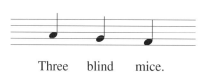

Three   blind   mice.

So far, things are pretty simple. In the "Three Blind Mice" example above, the music is written for a singer; you know this because lyrics appear beneath the notes. But you, whether a singer or not, can glean some important information about reading music from this short example.

What's important to realize is that a note on a staff gives you *two pieces of information at the same time.*

- It tells you the note's *pitch* (how high or low the note is). Notes get higher in pitch as they move higher on the staff and lower in pitch as they move lower on the staff.

- It tells you the note's *duration* (how long it is to be held). The different shapes of the notes signify whether they are long notes or short notes or somewhere in between.

In "Three Blind Mice," because the notes are all the same shape, they are held for the same amount of time. Mentally, or out loud if you wish, sing the lyrics "Three blind mice…" and notice that each word is held for one unit of time and that those units are of equal duration. If you understand all this, you're already reading music. Congratulations!

READING MUSIC IN THEORY VS. READING MUSIC IN PRACTICE

If you wanted to learn how to swim, you probably wouldn't do very well just by reading a book about it. You'd have to get in the water and move your arms and legs and practice for quite a while. It's pretty much the same thing with reading music. If you only read about it, without doing it on an instrument, you won't get very far. That's because in order to read music fluently, you have to understand at a glance the information the notes give about their pitch and duration.

Think about reading text. When you see a word, any word, you know instantly what it is. If you had to sound it out letter by letter, as a first grader might do, you would be a very slow reader. It's the same thing with reading music. You need to understand three things instantly when you look at music:

- How high or low the notes are, based on their position on the staff.

- How long or short the notes are, based on their shapes.

- Where to find those notes, or how to finger them, on an instrument.

ABOUT THE PIANO KEYBOARD

When most beginners start learning music—whether it's to play an instrument, or to learn about music theory, or to learn how to read music—they use the piano keyboard as a starting point. That's because (1) it's visually conducive; you can see all the notes at once and (2) it's easy to play because, as J. S. Bach once pointed out about keyboard instruments, all you have to do is hit the right note at the right time and the instrument plays itself!

So, rather than simply read about how to read music, you should play all the examples in this book on a piano keyboard, either acoustic or electric. If you don't own one, you should borrow one or buy one. New electronic keyboards can be found for less than $50. However, because this isn't a book about how to play the piano, per se, we won't dwell on fingering and technique and so on. We'll give you just the information you need to play the examples on the instrument.

CHAPTER 2

ABOUT PITCH, PART 1

MORE ABOUT THE STAFF

The five lines of the staff are numbered from 1–5, with the bottom one called the *first line* and the top one called the *fifth line:*

The staff consists not only of its five lines but also of the four spaces between the lines. These are numbered from 1–4, with the bottom one called the *first space* and the top one called the *fourth space:*

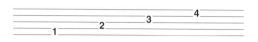

MORE ABOUT THE PITCHES OF NOTES

Every note has a letter name, depending on where it falls on the staff; that is, which line it sits on or which space it sits in. Only the first seven letters of the alphabet—A, B, C, D, E, F, G—are used in naming notes, with each letter higher in pitch than the letter that precedes it. So, if you move from A to B to C, you are moving higher in pitch, and the notes move higher on the staff. Conversely, if you move from C to B to A, you are moving lower in pitch and the notes move lower on the staff.

What if you want to play the next note higher than G? Think about the numbers on the face of a clock. If you start at 1 and go to 12 and then continue, you come to 1 again. The same principle applies to the musical letter names. After G, you come to A again. So, a longer series of ascending notes might look like this: A, B, C, D, E, F, G, A, B, C, D, E, F, G, A, B, C…

Moving in a downward direction, the next note below A is G again. So, a long series of descending notes might look like this: G, F, E, D, C, B, A, G, F, E, D, C, B, A, G, F, E…

Of course, it's not enough to simply recognize the letter names of notes by their position on the staff. You also need to know (pretty much instantly) where to find them on an instrument—on a piano keyboard for the purposes of this book. And that comes from practice, some hands-on "doing"!

MORE ABOUT THE SHAPES OF NOTES

If the letter names tell you the pitches of the notes and you know where to find those pitches/letters on the piano keyboard, why doesn't written music consist of just letter names? Well, some people do notate very simple music with letter names. But letter names don't give you any information about rhythm; they don't tell you how *long* to hold the notes. That's where the different shapes of notes come in.

You may know that all notes have a rounded portion—called the note's *head*—that sits on a line or in a space, but sometimes the head is hollow and sometimes solid; and usually there are vertical lines (called *stems*) connected to the note head, and sometimes there are little doohickeys (called *flags* and *beams*) attached to the stems. Each particular variation signifies a certain type of note, with names like *whole note, half note, quarter note, eighth note,* and *16th note.* And, as your inner mathematician can imagine, a whole note lasts (is held, or sustained) twice as long as a half note, which lasts twice as long as a quarter note, which lasts twice as long as an eighth note, which lasts twice as long as a 16th note. Sometimes you may even see a very short note called a *32nd note,* which lasts half as long as a 16th note. But more on rhythm later; for now, we're concentrating on pitch.

EVERYTHING IS RELATIVE: ABOUT CLEFS

A staff by itself has no real meaning until you know which lines and spaces signify which letters. The tricky part is that some instruments (for example, the piano, the organ, and the harp) generally use more than one staff for their written music, one staff for high notes, played by the right hand, and another for low notes, played by the left hand. And the letter names indicated by the staff lines and spaces for the right hand staff are *different* from those indicated by the left hand staff. So, how do you know which lines indicate which letters?

A symbol called a *clef* is written at the beginning (the left edge—because music is read from left to right) of the staff, and the clef indicates that a certain staff line represent a certain letter. The clef used by the right hand of the piano (and for a lot of other instruments, such as flute, violin, and guitar) is called the *G* clef, or the *treble* clef. It's called the *G* clef because the clef itself looks a little like a stylized capital *G.* It's also known as the *treble* clef because it's used for a staff that represents notes that are rather high. In music, the word *treble* refers to notes than are high, as opposed to *bass,* which refers to notes that are low.

As seen in the example below, the G clef appears to wrap around the second line of the staff. Because it's called the G clef and it wraps around the second line, it indicates that the second line of the staff (as a reminder, that's the second line from the *bottom*) is indeed a G note.

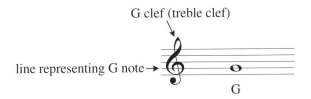

Given that the second line is G, you can now determine all the other letter names of the *treble staff* (a staff with a treble clef) because as you move up to the next consecutive line or space, the letters get higher; and as you move down to the next consecutive line or space, the letters get lower:

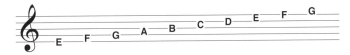

You know that a note on the second line of the treble staff is a G, but how do you know where to play that G on the piano. Even if you already know the names of the various white keys of the piano, you may not know which of several Gs on the piano to play.

ABOUT THE PIANO KEYBOARD

A piano keyboard consists of white keys and black keys, with the black keys organized into repeating groups of twos and threes.

As composer/author Blake Neely points out in his book *Piano for Dummies,* each group of two black keys looks kind of like a pair of chopsticks (which happens to start with the letter *C*), and each group of three black keys looks kind of like the prongs of a fork (which happens to start with the letter *F*). So, the white key immediately to the left of each group of *two* black keys is a *C* (as in *chopsticks*), and the white key immediately to the left of each group of *three* black keys is an *F* (as in *fork*):

Once you know how to find C and F on the keyboard, you can determine the letter names of the other white keys by knowing that the keys proceed in alphabetical order, letter by letter, ascending to the right and descending to the left. So, the two white keys directly above C are *D* and *E,* and the three white keys directly above F are *G, A,* and *B:*

ABOUT MIDDLE C

On a keyboard, the C note (or key) that's closest to the middle of the keyboard is known as (not surprisingly) *middle C:*

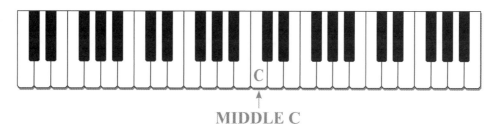

The G staff line that's indicated by the treble clef is the first G above middle C:

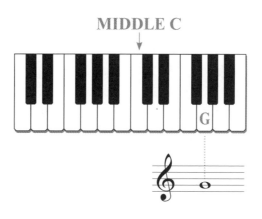

We can now correlate all the notes on the treble staff with the white keys of the piano keyboard:

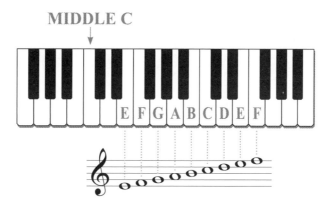

ABOUT THE BASS CLEF

For notes that are low, such as notes played by the left hand on the piano (or by such instruments as bassoon, trombone, and cello), a staff with an *F* clef, or *bass* clef, is used. It's called an F clef because it (supposedly) looks like a stylized capital *F* (with two dots after it). And it's also known as a *bass* clef because it's used to indicate notes that are low. As stated, the word *bass* refers to notes that are low. The dots of the F clef sit above and below the fourth line of the staff, indicating that that line is an F:

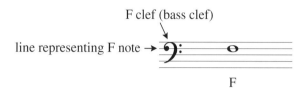

By moving upward and downward from F, you can now determine all the letter names of the bass staff:

The F note indicated by the bass clef, the fourth line of the bass staff, is the first F below middle C:

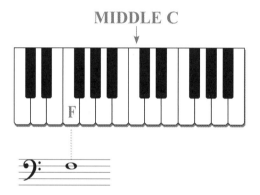

You can now correlate all the notes on the bass staff with the white keys of the piano keyboard.

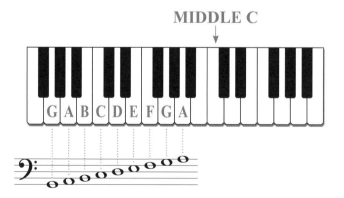

MEMORIZING THE PITCHES OF THE STAFF

The treble and bass *staves* (plural of *staff*) have five lines and four spaces each, for a total of 18 pitches. That's quite a few lines/pitches to memorize. And in order to read music fluently, you need to be able to recognize the letter name of each line and space as easily as you can recite the alphabet or count to ten.

An aid to memorization is a phrase or word that helps you easily identify the letter names of the lines or spaces. For the lines for the treble staff—E, G, B, D, F—students have long relied on the phrase "Every Good Boy Does Fine":

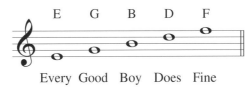

And for the spaces of the treble staff—F-A-C-E—they think of the word *face*:

For the lines of the bass staff—G, B, D, F, A—the phrase "Good Boys Do Fine Always" or "Great Big Dogs Fight Animals" has been used:

And for the spaces of the bass staff—A, C, E, G—you can think of the phrase "All Cars Eat Gas" or "All Cows Eat Grass":

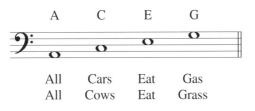

Of course, simply saying these phrases won't necessarily make you recognize the names/pitches of the staff lines and spaces as easily as you recognize the words on this page, but after practicing a while—putting what you know into practice by reading music and playing it on the keyboard—the identification of the lines and spaces, and where to find those notes on the keyboard, will indeed become second nature.

STARTING TO READ MUSIC

You now know enough about recognizing pitches on a staff and finding those pitches on a piano keyboard to read some music. Below is the beginning of a well-known children's song. Play it on a piano keyboard with your right hand, using whichever fingers feel comfortable to you. If you have trouble remembering which notes the lines and spaces of the treble staff represent, think of the phrase "Every Good Boy Does Fine" for the lines and of the word FACE for the spaces. By using that trick, you see right away that the letter names, from left to right, are C-C-C-G-A-A-G (starting with the first C to the right of middle C). By the way, concerning rhythm: your familiarity with the song "Old MacDonald Had a Farm" lets you know that all the notes are of the same duration; but even if you were unfamiliar with the song, you'd know the notes are all of the same duration simply because they are all of the same shape.

Old Mac - Don - ald   had   a   farm...

Now play the same melody from a different starting pitch. The letter names in this example are D-D-D-A-B-B-A. By the way, you may notice that some of the notes have their *stems*, the vertical lines connected to the note heads, pointing up while others have them pointing down. What's important to know is that the direction of the stem doesn't affect the duration of the note. Simply for the sake of not taking up more page space than necessary, notes above the middle line generally have their stems pointing down, and notes below the middle line generally have them pointing up. Technically, the stem of a note on the middle line itself can point either way, but it generally points down.

Now play the same melody from yet another starting pitch. The letter names in this example are F-F-F-C-D-D-C. Again, think of "Every Good Boy Does Fine" for the lines and FACE for the spaces if you need help remembering which notes the lines and spaces represent.

Now, reading the bass clef, use your left hand, with whichever fingers feel comfortable, to play the same melody yet again. To help you remember which notes the lines and spaces of the bass staff represent, think of the phrase "Good Boys Do Fine Always" or "Great Big Dogs Fight Animals" for the lines and either "All Cars Eat Gas" or "All Cows Eat Grass" for the spaces. Using this trick, you see right away that the letter names are C-C-C-G-A-A-G, starting with the first C to the left of middle C.

Now, still using your left hand, start the melody from D, as shown below. The notes are D-D-D-A-B-B-A, starting one white key higher than in the previous example.

Finally, play the melody from F, the first F below middle C. The notes are now F-F-F-C-D-D-C.

EXTENDING THE STAFF

Each consecutive line and space of the staff, whether treble or bass, is known as a *step,* or a *degree.* If you start from the first (bottom) line of the staff and move up to the first space, you're moving up *one step,* or *one degree.* The letter names of the staff make it apparent that this is so. Taking the treble staff as an example, moving from the bottom line to the first space takes you from E to F, which is the distance of one letter name (or one step, or degree).

Likewise, if you move from the first space up to the second line, you're moving up one step, or degree. And if you move from the first line to the second line, skipping over the first space (or from the first space to the second space, skipping over the second line), you're moving *two* steps, or degrees. Again, the letter names of the treble staff demonstrate this: From line 1 to line 2 is E to G (a distance of two letter names, or steps, or degrees), and from space 1 to space 2 is F to A (again a distance of two letter names, or steps, or degrees).

The staff itself consists of only nine degrees, represented by the five lines and the four intervening spaces. But in reality, more than nine notes are used; that is, notes higher and lower than those nine are used. To indicate these notes that are higher or lower than the nine degrees of the staff, music *notators* (composers, arrangers, and others who write music on paper) extend the staff by drawing short additional lines, called *ledger lines* (sometimes spelled *leger* lines), above and below the staff itself, as shown below.

Ledger lines

These ledger lines extend the staff by creating additional degrees, additional lines and spaces, above and below the staff. So, knowing that the top line of the treble staff is F, you can now determine the letter names of notes above that F indicated by ledger lines and by the spaces between them.

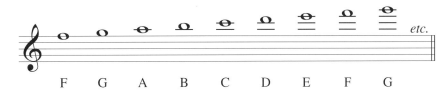

Similarly, you can determine the letter names of the notes indicated by ledger lines below the bottom line of the treble staff.

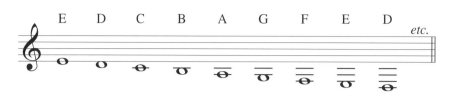

The figure below shows how all the notes of the treble staff, including high and low notes indicated by ledger lines, relate to the piano keyboard.

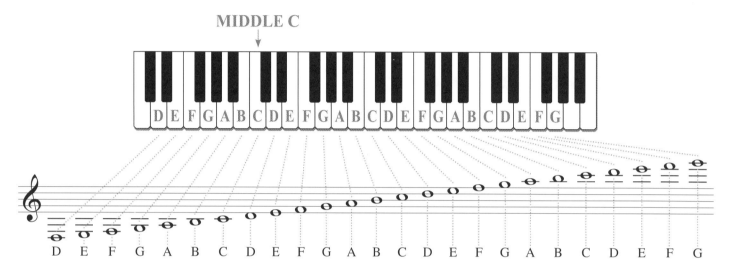

Ledger lines are used to extend the range of the bass staff as well. For notes above the top line A, you have B, C, D, and so on, as shown below.

Extending the bass staff downward, below bottom line G, you have F, E, D, and so on, as shown below.

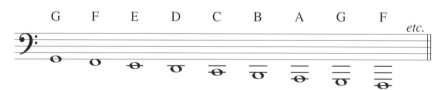

The figure below shows how all the notes of the bass staff, including high and low notes indicated by ledger lines, relate to the piano keyboard.

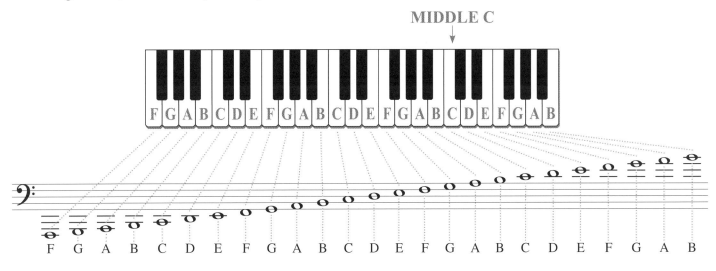

READING MUSIC WITH LEDGER LINES

The example below, which employs ledger lines above the treble staff, is another famous song whose opening notes are all of the same duration. Play this one on the piano, using your right hand with any fingering that feels comfortable. The first note, in the first imaginary space above the treble staff, is the second G to the right of middle C, as you easily can see by taking a look at the example on the previous page that correlates the notes of the treble staff to the keyboard.

Yan - kee Doo - dle went to town...

Using your right hand, play the same melody in a lower range by reading ledger lines *below* the treble staff. The first note, in the third imaginary space below the treble staff, is the G below middle C.

Now, using your left hand, play yet another famous song whose opening notes are all of the same duration by reading ledger lines above the *bass* staff. The first note, G, is within the staff (G below middle C), and the second note (on the second ledger line above the staff) is the first E above middle C (as can be seen in the example above that correlates the notes of the bass staff to the keyboard).

Dash - ing through the snow...

Again with the left hand, play the same melody in a lower range by reading ledger lines *below* the bass staff. The first note, on the second ledger line below the bass staff, is the C two octaves below middle C. An *octave* is a distance of eight steps, or degrees—as from any key to the next key, above or below, of the same letter name; for example, from any C to the next C above or below, or from any D to the next D above or below, and so on.

THE GRAND STAFF

Until now we've been reading music to be played on the piano one hand and one staff at a time. But piano music is generally written on a double-staff system known as a *grand staff*. The grand staff, as seen below, consists of both a treble staff and a bass staff, and these are joined at the left by a vertical line and a curved brace, or bracket. Notes appearing on the treble staff are usually played by the right hand, and those on the bass staff by the left.

treble staff

bass staff

The example below shows the notes from C below middle C to C above middle C on a grand staff, and where these notes are found on the keyboard.

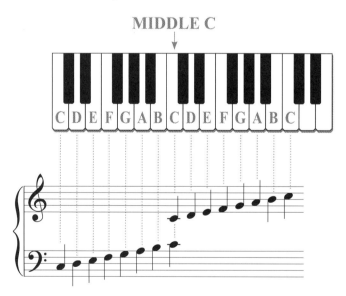

In the example above you see that middle C is notated, with the use of a single ledger line, on *both* staves. It can be played by either hand. But middle C isn't the only note that can be notated on either staff. With the use of ledger lines, many notes around the center of the keyboard can be notated on both staffs, as seen below.

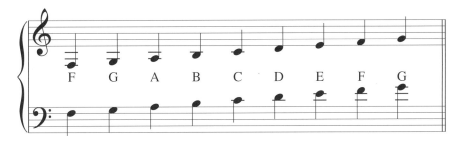

Even more notes can be notated on either staff, depending on how many ledger lines a notator is willing to use. The chart below shows a five-octave range of notes on both the grand staff and the keyboard in which 13 notes are notated on both staves. *Suggestion:* Make a mental note of this page number for future reference, as when you need to find where any particular note on the staff is located on the keyboard.

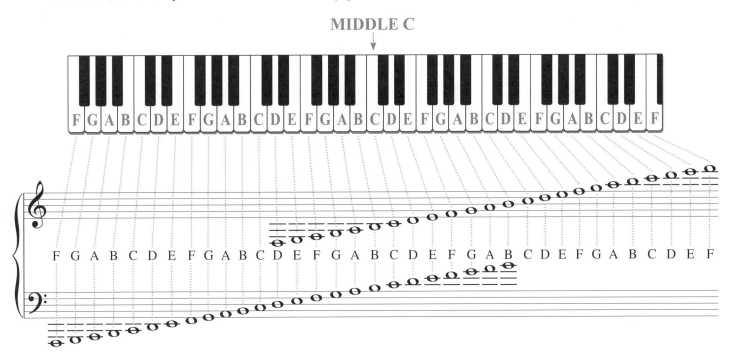

Earlier, you played simple tunes with one hand. Now try playing them by reading notes on the grand staff and using both hands, right hand for treble staff notes and left hand for bass staff notes. First is "Old MacDonald Had a Farm," two times—starting first from F above middle C, then from G above middle C.

Next is "Yankee Doodle" using both hands. Play it twice—first from middle C, then from G below middle C.

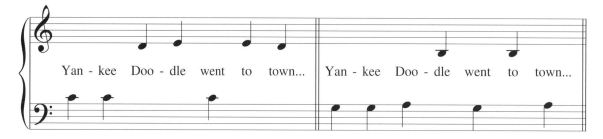

Finally, play "Jingle Bells" with both hands, two times—first from G below middle C, then from D below middle C.

By playing the three examples above, you're reading and playing music the way it's done on a keyboard instrument; that is, you're reading notes on the grand staff and using two hands to play it.

This is how piano music is generally notated and played. As we move forward, for the purposes of introducing particular principles, if a single staff will suffice to demonstrate the principle, we'll use just a single staff. Keep in mind that most musical principles apply to either staff, and that music for piano is generally notated on a grand staff. On the other hand, music for many other instruments (flute, clarinet, oboe, bassoon, trumpet, French horn, trombone, tuba, violin, viola, cello, bass, and guitar) is notated on a *single* staff.

CLEF CHANGES AND OCTAVE SIGNS

Because it becomes difficult for readers to decipher notes that use many ledger lines, notators usually rely on other means to show very high and very low notes. For instance, in the example below, the first half shows music with many ledgers lines; the second half shows how a notator using a single staff might write the same music, by means of simply changing clefs.

What's important to realize about the example above is that it is permissible to change clefs by writing a new (different) clef somewhere in the middle of a line of music. All the notes following the clef change relate to the new clef rather than the original. In the example above, the second half uses fewer ledger lines than the first half.

The next example shows how notators avoid excessive ledger lines below the staff by changing from treble clef to bass clef in the middle of a passage. The first half uses no clef change and excessive ledger lines while the second half neatly avoids hard-to-read notes.

Each of the examples above could have been written without excessive ledger lines and with no clef change simply by beginning with a different clef. If the first of the two examples above started and remained in treble clef, then no more than two ledger lines (two for the opening A note) would be required. Likewise, if the second of the two examples started and remained in bass clef, only one ledger line would be required (for the opening D and C notes).

It is up to the notator to choose clefs in a way that makes the music as easy to read as possible. Also observe that the concept of the clef change within a passage applies both to single-staff music and to each of the individual staves of the piano's grand staff. You may sometimes see the upper staff of the piano's grand staff (the right hand's staff) written in *bass* clef, and sometimes see the lower staff of the grand staff (the left hand's staff) written in *treble* clef.

Another way notators avoid an excessive number of ledger lines is by means of "octave signs." These are symbols that show that a certain passage of music is to be played an octave (eight degrees) higher or lower than written. In the example below ("Jingle Bells" again), the symbol *8va* (pronounced *eight-V-A*) with a dashed line after it shows that the music encompassed by the dashed line is to be played an octave higher than written; instead of beginning *one* octave above middle C, begin the passage *two* octaves above. The second half of the example shows how the music would look without the use of an octave sign; you can see right away that it is difficult to read.

The symbol *8va* (which is an abbreviation of the Italian word *ottava,* meaning "octave") is used in the treble clef; it isn't used in the bass clef because in the bass clef a notator, writing on a single staff, will simply switch to treble clef (in the middle of a passage) to show higher notes, making ledger lines unnecessary; or, the notator might write the high notes of a piano piece's left hand part on the *upper* staff of the grand staff, with an indication (such as *L.H.)* that the notes in question are to be played by the left hand rather than the right.

Excessive ledger lines below the bass clef can be avoided by use of the symbol *8vb*, an abbreviation of the Italian *ottava bassa,* meaning "at the octave below." Again using the opening notes of "Jingle Bells," the example below shows how the music looks with the use of the *8vb* symbol and its dashed line (both placed below, not above, the staff), then without the *8vb* (again, an excessive number of ledger lines is hard to read). Play the example beginning from the D that's *three,* not two, Ds below middle C.

The symbol *8vb* is used in the bass clef; it isn't used in the treble clef because a notator will simply switch to bass clef for low notes that would require too many ledger lines; or, on a grand staff, the notator might write the low notes of the right-hand part on the lower staff of the grand staff with an indication, such as *R.H.,* that the notes in question are to be played by the right hand.

You now know how to read and play an extremely wide range of white-key notes on the keyboard. *A point of interest:* The white-key notes (as opposed to the black-key notes) are called *natural notes,* and, as previously noted, they're represented by the letters A, B, C, D, E, F, and G. By the way, the familiar sound of a major scale—that is, the familiar sound of *do-re-mi-fa-sol-la-ti-do*—corresponds to the white keys of the keyboard played consecutively from any C up to the next C. That pattern of notes, C-D-E-F-G-A-B-C, is known as the *C major scale;* and the major scale starting from C is the only major scale that uses white keys exclusively; all the other major scales, those starting from notes other than C, use at least one black key. Owing to its absence of black-key notes, the *key of C,* also known as the *key of C major* (music whose "home base" is the C note and that primarily uses notes derived from the C major scale for its melody and harmony), is generally used as a starting point for musical instruction.

But before moving on to how to read and play the black keys on the piano, we'll take a look at music's other main aspect (other than pitch, that is)—*rhythm.* In the section that follows, you will learn how to read and play various rhythms by understanding the timing of the various note shapes.

A BIT MORE ABOUT CLEFS

The primary purpose of choosing one clef over another is to make the notes fit on the staff nicely, without an excessive number of ledger lines. As mentioned, the piano generally uses the treble clef for upper staff of the grand staff and the bass clef for the lower staff. Other instruments use either the treble *or* the bass clef (on a single staff), depending on whether their range happens to be high (flute, clarinet, trumpet, violin) or low (bassoon, trombone, cello).

Some instruments, usually referred to as *transposing instruments,* automatically sound a note that's different from the one indicated on the printed page. Some transposing instruments sound an octave higher or lower than indicated; for example, the piccolo sounds an octave higher than indicated on paper, and the guitar and the double bass (also called *stand-up bass, bass violin, bass fiddle,* or simply *bass*) sound an octave lower than indicated. Still other instruments automatically sound a pitch that's a completely different letter name from the written pitch; such instruments include the clarinet, saxophone, trumpet, and French horn.

Although today we mostly use two clefs, treble and bass, in centuries past (as in the time of J. S. Bach, for example), several more clefs were used, especially for vocal parts. Each of the various vocal ranges—that is, soprano, alto, tenor, and bass—had its own clef. These were called *soprano clef, alto clef,* and so on. This was for the purpose of minimizing the number of ledger lines that might be necessary. You already know about the bass clef. The other three clefs mentioned—soprano clef, alto clef, and tenor clef—are known as *C clefs,* because their clef symbols are shaped (supposedly) like a letter C; the clef is positioned around (or centered upon) a particular line of the staff, thus signifying that line as middle C.

In the soprano clef, the clef symbol is centered upon the bottom (first) line of the staff, indicating that that line is middle C; in the alto clef, the clef surrounds the middle (third) line, indicating that line as middle C; and in the tenor clef, the clef is positioned around the fourth line, indicating that line as middle C. This is illustrated below.

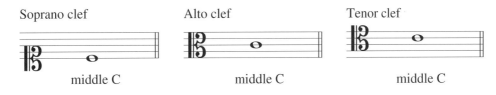

Soprano clef   Alto clef   Tenor clef

middle C   middle C   middle C

Today, the soprano clef is no longer used, but the tenor clef is useful for notating especially high notes on the bassoon, trombone, or cello—all normally written in bass clef. The alto clef is used for viola music. (The viola is an instrument that looks like a violin but is a bit larger and sounds a bit lower). Below is how the natural notes from G below middle C to G above middle C look in treble clef, alto clef (for viola players), and bass clef. Now you can see why Bach liked to notate music for singers with an alto range (from around G below middle C to C above middle C) in alto clef rather than in treble or bass clef—fewer ledger lines!

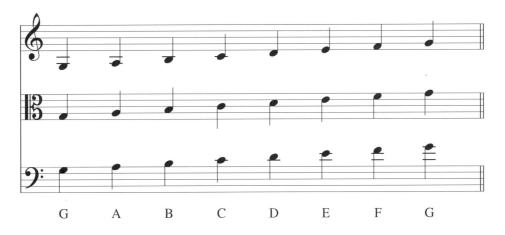

G   A   B   C   D   E   F   G

CHAPTER 3

ABOUT RHYTHM, PART 1

When you read and play the rhythmic aspect of music, which pertains to durations rather than pitch, you're dealing with two rhythms at the same time. The first is the *beat,* or the *pulse,* of the music. That's what you tap your foot to in a steady pattern, or feel in your bones, when you listen to music. The important point about the beat is that, except in special situations, it's steady and unchanging: TAP-TAP-TAP-TAP. It's so steady and unchanging, in fact, that you don't even have to count it consciously; it's just there, in the background, like your heartbeat.

The other rhythm is that of the individual written notes—whole notes, half notes, quarter notes, and so on. These are seldom steady and unchanging. In the previous chapter, the opening notes of "Old MacDonald Had a Farm," "Yankee Doodle," and "Jingle Bells" were steady and unchanging, just like the beat, and we used those examples to avoid having to deal with rhythmic complications too soon; but, as you know, in nearly all music the durations of the notes vary.

ABOUT NOTE VALUES

When you read rhythmic notation, you're *relating the written notes to the beat.* (More about what that means a bit later.) The first step is to recognize the various note values. Below is a chart that identifies these by name. As stated in Chapter 1, all notes have a rounded portion call the *head* or *note head*, which might be hollow or solid. Some have a vertical line, called a *stem,* that's attached to the head. Some have *flags* or *beams* attached to the head. In the chart, stems might point up or down; as stated, the direction has no effect on the duration of the note. Also, consecutive notes with flags can be grouped together, with *beams* replacing flags. This also does not affect the duration of the notes. In fact, in printed music, flagged notes generally *are* grouped together rather than indicated individually with flags. In some old printed music you're likely to see notes for singers—notes to be sung—flagged separately rather than beamed, because that was once common practice for vocal music.

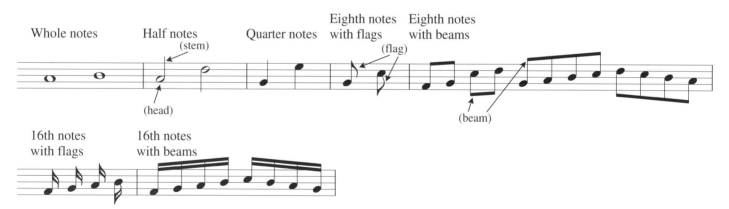

Notice that whereas eighth notes have single flags or beams, 16th notes have double flags or beams. Theoretically, we could extend the chart by showing even smaller (shorter) note values—that is, 32nd notes, with triple flags or beams, and even rarely used 64th notes, with quadruple flags and beams. As a reminder—and we pointed out that your inner mathematician will tell you this—a whole note lasts twice as long as a half note, which lasts twice as long as a quarter note, which last twice as long as an eighth note, and so on. You can see this visually in the chart that follows, which shows the relative value of notes. You'll note that some of the eighth and 16th notes are flagged while others are beamed; again, this doesn't affect the duration.

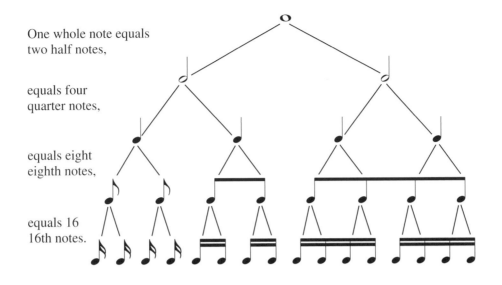

One whole note equals
two half notes,

equals four
quarter notes,

equals eight
eighth notes,

equals 16
16th notes.

ABOUT TIME SIGNATURES

Once you know how to identify, by sight, the various note values, your next step is to determine—by looking at the printed music you want to read—which of those note values (whole note or half note or quarter note or eighth note or 16th note) is the one that's being used to represent *one beat*—yes, that same beat that you tap your foot to, or snap your fingers to, or feel deep inside you.

Here's how it's done. At the beginning of the first line of music that you want to read, you'll see, after the clef, two numbers that look like a fraction; but it's not really a fraction because there's no middle dividing line between the numbers—what looks like a dividing line is simply the middle staff line. For example, you may see something that looks like one of the following fractions (but positioned vertically, with one over the other, rather than side by side, as appears here): 2/4, 3/4, 4/4, 3/8, 6/8, 9/8, 4/2, 2/2. Those numbers are called the music's *time signature*. In your mind, take the bottom number of the time signature and pretend that it's the bottom number of a fraction. Take, as an example, the first time signature mentioned above: 2/4. The bottom number is 4, so make that the bottom number of your hypothetical fraction. Then make the top number of your fraction a 1; you'll always make the top number a 1 when using this method to determine which note value represents the beat. You now have a fraction of 1/4, which is the same as *one quarter,* which tells you that it's the *quarter note* that represents the beat (or, as some people say, it's the quarter note that *receives* the beat).

What does it mean to say that the quarter note represents the beat? Look at the example below. If we know that a quarter note represents the beat, then each note of the written music, being a quarter note, is exactly one beat in duration. Play the melody indicated while tapping your foot in a steady pulse; play one note per foot-tap.

ABOUT BAR LINES AND MEASURES

When you look at printed music, you see vertical lines that extend from the bottom line of the staff to the top line, after every few beats. These are called *bar lines*. Here's how the previous example looks with bar lines added.

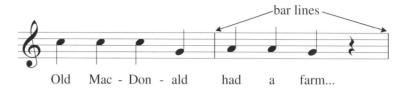

Old   Mac - Don - ald   had   a   farm...

In the example above, the squiggly symbol just before the second bar line is a *rest*, meaning that you don't play on that beat; you *rest*. We'll talk more about rests later on. The music between the bar lines is called a *measure* (or a *bar*; the terms are interchangeable), as illustrated below.

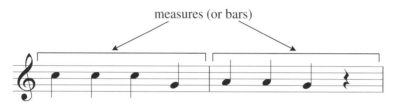

Note that the brackets above the measures in the example above wouldn't appear in real music; they're used in the example merely for demonstration purposes.

Why is music broken up into measures, by means of vertical bar lines? There are two reasons. First, the measures divide the music into small chunks that are easier to deal with (easier to process mentally) than is one long, extended passage. Think of it this way: When you tell someone your phone number, you usually divide it up into three little chunks; for example, instead of saying 2125551234, you say 212-555-1234, making the information easier to process for the listener by dividing it into small sections.

To understand the other reason music is divided into measures, we need to talk a little more about time signatures. You know that the bottom number of the time signature tells you which note value represents the beat. The *top* number of the time signature tells you *how many beats will appear within each measure*; that is, how many beats will appear in between any two consecutive bar lines. This is illustrated below.

Top number 4 tells you that each
measure will contain four beats.

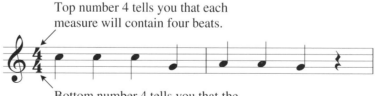

Bottom number 4 tells you that the
quarter note represents one beat.

By dividing music into measures, the notator is not only making the music easier for you to process by dividing it into small sections, he's also telling you which notes of the music should be stressed more than the others. What does this mean? Certain kinds of music naturally divide themselves into a certain number of beats. For example, a march is used to accompany a left-right foot motion, as in "LEFT-right, LEFT-right," and so on. Because the foot motion (LEFT-right) consists of *two* steps, march music is written in 2/4 time (*two* beats per measure, with the *quarter note* receiving the beat). But whenever you say "LEFT-right," you naturally stress the first beat; that is, you say, or feel, LEFT-right rather than left-RIGHT." That's what we mean by stressing a note. In this example, the first beat is stressed, and the second beat is unstressed. *Stressed* and *unstressed* beats are sometimes called *strong* and *weak* beats, respectively.

What's important to realize about measures is that the first note of each measure is stressed. One more example: When people dance the waltz, they count ONE-two-three, ONE-two-tree, and so on, with the first count (the ONE) of each group stressed and the other counts unstressed. So, printed music for waltzes is written in 3/4 time—*three* beats per measure, with the quarter note receiving the beat.

For demonstration purposes, if we used the symbol > (called an *accent mark*) to indicate that a note is stressed, then the relative stresses of 2/4 time can be indicated like this:

And the relative stresses of 3/4 time can be indicated like this:

The relative stresses of 4/4 time (*four* beats per measure, with the quarter note receiving the beat) are a bit more complicated than those of 2/4 and 3/4 time because 4/4 time contains not only stressed and unstressed beats, but also a "slightly stressed" beat (the third beat), as in **ONE**-two-**three**-four, **ONE**-two-**three**-four, and so on (with bold capital letters representing a stress and bold lower case letters representing a slight stress). By using an accent mark in parentheses (>) to indicate a slightly stressed beat, we can demonstrate the relative stresses of 4/4 time, as below.

When you read and play the music for "Old MacDonald Had a Farm," you naturally give the music its proper stresses—"**OLD** Mac-**Don**-ald | **HAD** a **farm**"—because you're familiar with the song. But if you see music that you're not familiar with that's in 4/4 time, especially music without lyrics, you give the beats the same relative stresses— **ONE**-two-**three**-four.

A point of interest: 2/4 time and 3/4 time correspond to certain poetic meters that you may remember learning about when you studied poetry in school. *Trochaic* meter (stressed, unstressed) corresponds to 2/4, as in this line from Shakespeare's *Macbeth:* "**DOU**-ble, **DOU**-ble **TOIL** and **TROU**-ble." And *dactylic* meter (stressed, unstressed, unstressed) corresponds to 3/4 time, as in this line from Tennyson's "The Charge of the Light Brigade": "**CAN**-non to **RIGHT** of them, **CAN**-non to **LEFT** of them." Most likely, if one were to set these lines to music, the Shakespeare example would be written in 2/4 time and the Tennyson in 3/4 time.

MUSIC FOR PRACTICE

Play the three examples below on the keyboard. Each is a famous song, but we're not telling you what they are. Play the notes as written and see if you can identify the songs. The first one is in 2/4 time and begins on middle C (in treble clef). Use your right hand to play this example. Remember to stress the first beat of each measure (**ONE**-two, **ONE**-two). The last measure of the example contains a *half note;* because it lasts twice as long as a quarter note, you strike it on beat 1 and allow it to continue to sound (without restriking it) through beat 2. The double bar line at the end signifies the end of the example.

The next example is in 3/4 time, in bass clef. Use your left hand to play this one. Remember to stress the first beat of each measure (**ONE**-two-three, **ONE**-two-three). By the way, the first beat of each measure is referred to as the *downbeat*—that's because when a conductor conducts, he's moves his baton in a downward motion for the first beat of each measure. Note the half notes at the beginning of the third and fourth measures. Strike them on beat 1 and allow them to sound through beat 2. The last beat of the last measure is a rest, so don't play anything there.

The next example is in 4/4 time, in treble clef. Use your right hand, and give an emphasis to each down beat (beat 1), and a slight emphasis to beat 3 of each measure. For the half notes, strike on the beat indicated, and allow the note to sound through the following beat, without restriking.

You were probably able to determine that the songs above were, in order, "Frère Jacques," "Over the River and Through the Woods," and "Mary Had a Little Lamb." But in case you weren't, go over the examples again, correlating how the songs go in your mind, as when you sing them to yourself, with how they look on the page. If you imagine lyrics under the notes, you should have no trouble playing the songs.

MIXING UP THE TIME VALUES

The examples you've played so far have been relatively simple—because the notes in them were primarily quarter notes, which happened to receive the beat. But in real music, things get more complicated than "Frère Jacques" and "Mary Had a Little Lamb." All sorts of combinations of note values (quarters, eights, halves, and so on) are used.

The important point is that in each measure of music, the combined rhythmic value of all the notes must add up to the number of beats per measure, indicated by the top number of the time signature. In 4/4 time, for example, each measure will contain a total of *four* beats. Because you understand the relative value of notes, you realize that a measure of 4/4 time could be made up of four quarter notes (as in the first measure of the "Mary Had a Little Lamb" example), or two half notes, or one whole note, or eight eighth notes. But several *different* note values that together add up to four beats might be used within a measure; for example, you might have one half note and four eight notes; or one quarter note and six eighth notes; or one half note, one quarter note, and four 16th notes, or *any other combination*. The number of possibilities is practically endless.

It would be extremely difficult to read the rhythmic aspect of music if you tried to keep track of how long to hold each individual note; this is especially true when dealing with short notes, such as 16ths, each of which is held for only a quarter of a beat in any time signature whose bottom number is 4. So, musicians have a better way of reading rhythm. Instead of thinking about individual notes, they think in terms of *beats;* that is, they think about the sound of what happens *in each beat.* This concept is somewhat similar to how you read text—for example, the words on this page. You don't look at the individual letters; instead, you see and recognize full words. Think of notes as letters, and of beats as words. Taking the first four words of this sentence as an example, you're dealing with four words, not with 18 letters.

Likewise, in reading a measure filled with many notes, you can deal with four sounds (in 4/4 time) rather than with however many notes you might have in the measure—if you think in terms of *beats* rather than in terms of *individual notes.* And you do this *by memorizing the common sounds that can occur within a beat.* This is not hard to do because the number of common sounds within a beat is rather limited. For example, you can have (1) just one note being sounded on the beat, as in each of the beats of the first measure of "Old MacDonald Had a Farm" or "Mary Had a Little Lamb," or (2) nothing being struck within the beat (that is, a rest, or a continuation of a previously struck note), or (3) two notes being struck, one after the other, or (4) four consecutive notes being struck. Of course, there are other combinations that we'll get to later, but these are the most common, and their sounds are not hard to learn.

How can you learn these sounds? Here's a gimmick that might be helpful. Pretend you want to make a sandwich with two slices of bread, cream cheese, and peanut butter. Now, tap you foot in a rather slow but steady rhythm; these foot-taps represent beats. Tap in 4/4 time, so give an emphasis to the first tap of each four taps (and a slight emphasis to the third tap), like this: **TAP**-tap-**tap**-tap | **TAP**-tap-**tap**-tap, and so on. Now, say each element of the sandwich aloud, one after the other, each time your foot comes down, like this: (1) **bread**, (2) **bread, (3) cream** cheese, (4) **pea**nut butter. The sound of "bread," which is one syllable, corresponds to the sound of a quarter note in 4/4 time. The sound of "cream cheese" (two syllables) corresponds to the sound of two eighth notes played within a beat, and the sound of "pea-nut but-ter" (four syllables) corresponds to the sound of four 16th notes played within a beat.

Here's how our musical sandwich looks on paper:

So, if you're reading music in 4/4 time (or 2/4 or 3/4) and you see four 16th notes in a beat, rather than thinking to yourself that you have to hold each note for 25 percent of a beat, think of the sound of "peanut butter" and simply play that sound for that beat. If you see two eighth notes, you can think of the sound "cream cheese" and play that sound. It's important that you memorize these rhythmic sounds so that when you see them you can play them automatically, without even thinking about it.

Of course, you don't have to use the terms *bread, cream cheese,* and *peanut butter* to help you memorize the sounds of one quarter note, two eighth notes, and four 16th notes. Any words or phrases of the correct number of syllables can be used—whatever strikes your fancy. If, for example, instead of using foods we used trees and shrubs, we might have relied on the words *oak, maple,* and *huckleberry.* But you get the point—think of the overall sound of what happens in the beat rather than thinking of the individual notes.

Below are two examples that let you see how these rhythms look in actual use. First is "Baa! Baa! Black Sheep." You can play this on the keyboard or simply sing it in your mind. But pay attention to what happens in each beat; that is, do you hit once (quarter note; bread) or twice (two eighth notes; cream cheese) or four times (four 16th notes; peanut butter)? This one's in 2/4 time, so count two beats per measure.

The next example, "Hot Cross Buns," is also in 2/4 time, but here you have two consecutive beats of four 16th notes; it looks rather advanced, but because you've memorized the sound of four notes in a beat (peanut butter or huckleberry), it's simple to read and play. By the way, for fun, if you substitute our sandwich lyrics for the actual lyrics, you get: "Cream cheese, bread, | cream cheese, bread, | peanut but-ter, pea-nut but-ter, | cream cheese, bread." If it helps you to substitute those lyrics to help you read the music, go ahead and do so.

ABOUT RESTS

We've previously mentioned that a symbol called a *rest* indicates that you don't play, for the duration of the particular rest in question. In previous examples you've seen rests, the squiggly-shaped things, that last for one beat in 4/4 time. Every note value has a rest that corresponds to it, in name and in duration. So, there is a *half rest,* which lasts as long as a half note; a *quarter rest,* which lasts as long as a quarter note, and so on. But the *whole rest* is a special case—it always last for an entire measure, regardless of the time signature, so a silence for a full measure of 2/4 time is indicated by a *whole* rest, even though the note that lasts for a full measure in 2/4 time is the *half* note. The example below shows how each of the rests looks on the staff.

Whole rest   Half rest   Quarter rest   Eighth rest   16th rest

For now, let's take a look at the whole rest, half rest, and quarter rest in action; we'll get to the other rests later. In the two previous examples, you dealt with three different sounds, which you memorized: the sound of a single attack in a beat (the quarter note; bread), the sound of two attacks in a beat (two eighth notes; cream cheese), and the sound of four attacks in a beat (four 16th notes; peanut butter). But there's another possibility you already know about that can happen in a beat: no attack at all. Be aware that there are *two* ways that no attack can be indicated. One is by writing a note value that's longer than a beat; for example, if you see a half note in 2/4 time (equivalent in length to two beats), you hit on beat 1, but you don't hit on beat 2—*because the half note is sustained throughout that beat.* Another way to indicate that there is to be no attack on a certain beat is to write a *rest* on that beat. When there's a rest, you don't sustain a previously struck note; you have silence, which means lifting your hand off the keyboard.

In the example below, you deal with the "bread" and "cream cheese" sounds, as before, but you also deal with beats that have no attack—both as a continuation of a previously struck note (as in beat 2 of measure 2) and as a rest (as the one-beat rest, or *quarter rest,* in measures 1 and 5, the two-beat rest, or *half rest,* in measure 2, and the full-measure rest, or *whole rest,* in measure 4). Note that where there is no attack we put the beat numbers in parentheses. Play this one on the keyboard with your right hand, counting out the beats carefully and steadily, using the sounds of "bread," "cream cheese," and *no attack* in all the appropriate places. Note that at the beginning of measure 2, the "bread" sound will be more like "breeaad" because, although you attack only once, on beat 1, you hold the sound through the end of beat 2.

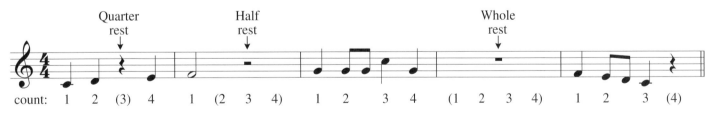

What complicates the reading of rhythmic notation is that sometimes short notes of unequal proportions are combined to make up a beat; for example, you might have an eighth note followed by two 16ths, or two 16ths followed by an eighth. And, to make matters worse, sometimes small rests are interspersed among the notes. But again, instead of trying to keep track of the durations of individual short notes and rests, you memorize the sounds of several more combinations of short notes (and of short notes and short rests), then you apply those memorized sounds beat by beat. But more on that later. Now it's time to return to the consideration of reading pitch. In the next section you'll learn, among other things, about playing the piano's black keys.

CHAPTER 4

ABOUT PITCH, PART 2

In Chapter 2 you learned how to identify the white keys, also called the *natural* notes, of the piano—both on the keyboard itself and on the music staff. And you learned that those white keys have names: A, B, C, D, E, F, and G. But what are the names of the black keys? Interestingly, the black keys don't have names of their own.

ABOUT THE BLACK KEYS; SHARPS AND FLATS

Often, when something doesn't have a name all its own, a kind of "fake name" is given to it by taking the real name of something similar and then modifying that name slightly. For example, a grade on a test that's higher than a B but lower than an A can be called a *B-plus* or an *A-minus.* Naming the black keys on the piano is done in a similar fashion. Consider the black key that sits between C and D. It's a little above C, but a little below D. So you might think that key would be called either C-plus or D-minus. And that's almost correct. That black key is called either *C-sharp* or *D-flat.*

Some necessary technical information: We've mentioned that the lines and spaces of the staff can be called *degrees,* or *steps*; that is, you move one degree, or step, when you move from any line to the space immediately above or below, or from any space to the line immediately above or below. We've also talked about the major scale, each note of which can be called a degree, or step. So, for example, in the C major scale (C, D, E, F, G, A, B, C), if you move from C to D, or from D to E, or from E to F, you're moving one step. But there are two different kinds of steps. One is called the *half step,* also sometimes called a *semitone,* which is the distance from any key on the piano to the very next key above or below. So, from E to F, with no black key in between, is a half step. And from C to the black key immediately above—or from D to the black key immediately below—is a half step. The other type of step is the *whole step,* also sometimes called a *tone,* which is equivalent to two half steps; or, to put it another way, it's the distance from any key to another key, above or below, that's *two* keys away. So, from C to D, with a black key in between, is a whole step. And from B to the black key immediately above C is a whole step. Take a look at your keyboard if you'd like to get a visual representation of the above, or to confirm that E to F really is a half step and C to D really is a whole step.

We said that the black key between C and D can be called *C-sharp* or *D-flat.* The term *sharp* indicates that the natural note/key to which "sharp" is attached should be played *one half step higher* than the natural note. So, if a C-sharp note is called for, you play the black key immediately above C. Likewise, if an F-sharp note is called for, you play the black key immediately above F. The musical symbol for a sharp—which is placed just before the note head of the natural note in question—looks kind of like a number sign: ♯. Below, as an example, is how F♯ above middle C looks on the keyboard and on the staff.

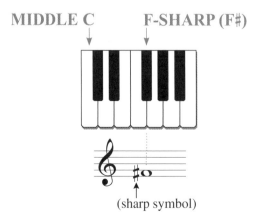

(sharp symbol)

The term *flat* indicates that the natural note/key to which "flat" is attached should be played *one half step lower* than the natural note. So, if a D-flat note is called for, you play the black key immediately below D. Likewise, if an A-flat note is called for, you play the black key immediately below A. The musical symbol for a flat—which is placed just before the note head of the natural note in question—looks kind of like a lower-case *b*. Below, as an example, is how A♭ above middle C looks on the keyboard and on the staff.

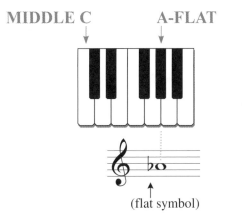

So, it should be apparent that every black key has two names—a "sharp" name based on the letter name of the white key below, and a "flat" name based on the letter name of the white key above. We can now name all the black keys, as shown in the figure below. By the way, when writing the names of black-key notes in text, you can either write out the word *sharp* or *flat,* as in *C-sharp* and *D-flat,* or you can simply write the appropriate musical symbol immediately after the letter, as in C♯ and D♭.

Now play a melody on the piano using only black keys. For this example we'll use sharps. Note that a sharp on a given note/letter applies to all notes of that degree that occur within the same measure. So, for the second and third Cs in measure 1, we don't rewrite the sharp symbols—but those Cs are indeed played as C♯s because the first sharp symbol of the measure applies to *all* the (third space) Cs. Hypothetically, if the melody contained a C in a higher or lower octave in that measure, then that C would require its own sharp symbol. We've written the letter names over the notes to emphasize the fact that all the Cs in the first measure are to be played as C♯s. We've also included lyrics under the notes—just in case you need help with the rhythm of the example, the Christmas classic "Up on the Housetop."

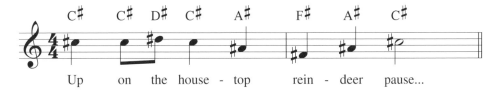

Now play the same melody, but by reading the black-key notes as *flats*. Just as with sharps, flats apply to all notes of the same degree within the same measure.

Now we'll combine white-key and black-key notes, using sharps, in the same example. Note that consecutive eighth notes can be beamed in groups of two or four; here we've grouped them in fours.

Now play the same melody a half step lower, reading the black-key notes as flats.

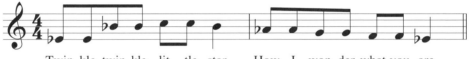

A technical matter: You may wonder how a music notator (composer, arranger) decides whether to notate black keys as sharps or flats. The decision depends on such factors as what key the piece is in (that is, what scale are the piece's notes derived from, and what is the "home base" note), what chord is being played to accompany the melody at the moment in question, and sometimes what direction the melody is going (upward or downward). But these are more the concerns of music theory than of music notation, and they are beyond the scope of this book. But if you're curious, check out any books or websites that focus on music theory. There you can learn all about *intervals* (distances between notes), different kinds of scales, harmony, and so on.

CANCELING A SHARP OR FLAT; THE NATURAL

Let's say we want to indicate that the first C of a measure is sharped (here we're using *sharp* as a verb, to mean "to raise by a half step"), but you want a subsequent C, of the same degree and in the same measure, to be played as a regular, white-key C (in other words, as the *natural* note C). This we achieve by means of a symbol, called a *natural*, or a *natural sign*, that cancels a previous sharp or flat on the same degree. The sign looks like a little parallelogram with the left side extending upward and the right side extending downward.

The example below shows how a natural cancels a sharp (measure 1) and a flat (measure 2). In measure 1, black-key G♯ moves down to white-key G-natural (also called simply G) thanks to the natural sign before the G on beat 3; and in measure 2, black-key A-flat moves up to white-key A, again thanks to the natural sign.

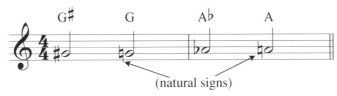

(natural signs)

The following example uses sharps, flats, and naturals. If you play it correctly, you'll recognize it as the opening melody of Tchaikovsky's "Dance of the Sugar Plum Fairy," from *The Nutcracker.* Use your right hand, and start playing on beat 2 of the first measure; beat 1 is a rest.

Now, using your left hand, play the same melody, but from a different starting pitch, by reading bass clef.

ABOUT KEYS SIGNATURES AND KEYS

We previously explained that the *key of C* is music whose "home base" is the C note and that primarily uses notes derived from the C major scale for its melody and harmony. And we pointed out that the *C major scale* is what you get if you play the white keys of the piano from C to C, the familiar sound of *do-re-mi-fa-sol-la-ti-do*. Likewise, the key of *any* particular letter name (the key of D, the key of E♭, the key of F♯, or whatever) is music whose "home base" is that pitch and that primarily uses notes from the major scale starting from that pitch.

A technical matter: The C major scale is the only major scale that uses white keys exclusively; all the others include one or more black keys. But what is the same about all major scales is their particular pattern of whole steps and half steps. Looking at the piano's white keys, you see that there are whole steps between them except for E-F and B-C; that is, except for E-F and B-C, there is an intervening black key between any two consecutive white keys. Knowing that, you see that the pattern of whole steps and half steps of the C major scale (the white keys, consecutively, from C up to the next C) is "whole-whole-half-whole-whole-whole-half." C to D is a whole step, D to E is a whole step, E to F is a half step, and so on. If you start at any given note and apply that pattern of whole and half steps, you create that note's major scale.

In order to read music, you don't have to know the exact pitches of all the major scales; that's more the concern of music theory than of music notation. But for the sake of demonstration, and in order to make our explanation of key signatures understandable, let's build a major scale from a note other than C. We'll start the scale from E♭. Applying the pattern of "whole-whole-half-whole-whole-whole-half" to the E♭ note, we get E♭-F-G-A♭-B♭-C-D-E♭. A quick look at the piano keyboard should confirm that this is so. By the way, in major scales, the letter names are always in alphabetical order, without skipping or repeating any letters; that's why we call the fourth and fifth notes of the E♭ major scale A♭ and B♭, not G♯ and A♯.

So, if we consider the concept of *the key of E♭* (also called *the key of E♭ major*), we understand that the "home base" note is E♭, and the music will consist primarily of notes from the E♭ major scale. That means that, in the written music, most or all of the Bs will be B♭s, the Es will be E♭s, and the As will be A♭s.

But a piece of music in the key of E♭ might have dozens, or even hundreds, of Bs and Es and As that need to be flatted. In order to make the written music less crowded and less busy-looking, and to save a lot of effort on behalf of the notator, we have a shortcut for indicating that certain notes in a piece are all to be flatted or all to be sharped. At the beginning of each line of music, after the clef, we write what's called a *key signature,* which is a group of flats or sharps—positioned on particular degrees of the staff—that apply *throughout a piece.* For example, we know that in the key of E♭, all Bs, Es, and As are flatted. In the example below you see the key signature for the key of E♭, on the piano's grand staff.

You see above that flats are positioned in the treble clef on third-line B, fourth-space E, and second-space A; and in the bass clef, they're positioned on second-line B, fourth-space E, and first-space A. But what's important to realize is that the flats in the key signature automatically apply to *all* the Bs, Es, and As in the piece, regardless of what degree of the staff (what octave, or range, or register) they happen to fall on. So, an E on the bottom line of the treble staff is automatically flatted, even though the flat symbol for E in the key signature is an octave higher than that, in the top space. The same concept applies to key signatures made up of sharps; that is, the sharps apply to all the notes in the piece of the letter names indicated by the sharps in the key signature, regardless of what degree of the staff they might fall on. Below is an example of a key signature made up of sharps—in this case two sharps, on F and C, which indicates the key of D major. That's because if you apply the major-scale pattern of whole and half steps to the D note, you get D-E-F♯-G-A-B-C♯-D.

If you see music with *no key signature,* that means the music has no pitches that are automatically sharped or flatted, which means that the music probably is based on the C major scale, and so probably is in the key of C.

Now that you understand how key signatures work, let's take another look at the "Twinkle, Twinkle, Little Star" example you played a bit earlier. We wrote the example in the key of E♭; that is, E♭ was the "home base" note and the music was based on notes from the E♭ major scale. By the way, the technical term for the "home base" note is the *tonic note,* or simply the *tonic*—which is the first note, or first degree, of any given scale. So, more correctly, we say that our "Twinkle, Twinkle, Little Star" example is in the key of E♭ and that E♭ is the tonic note. Here's how the music looked with flats written on all the applicable note, with no key signature given:

Now here's how that music would look in actual practice, with a key signature indicating the key of E♭; that is, with a signature of three flats—on B, E, and A:

As you see above, the key signature is written *before* the time signature. Also note that in music that continues long enough to require multiple lines, the key signature is repeated at the beginning of every line, but the time signature is written on the first line only.

The table below shows all the common key signatures for major keys. This is for reference only; you don't have to try to memorize it. Be aware that each of the signatures is derived from the sharped or flatted notes of the major scale of the same name as the key in question. For example, we saw earlier that the key of D has *two* sharps because the D major scale contains two sharps.

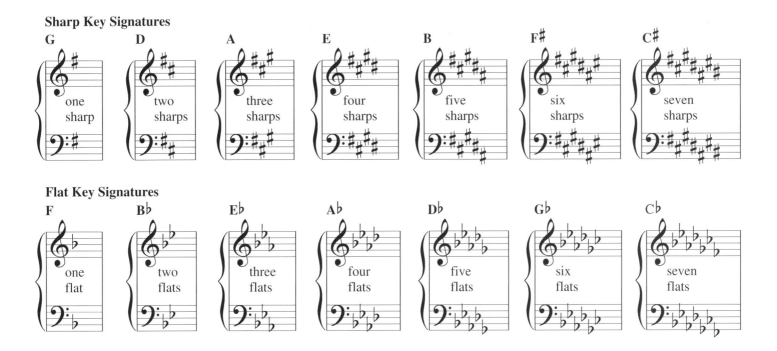

ABOUT ACCIDENTALS—SOME TERMINOLOGY

Each major key is made up of the notes of the major scale of the same name as that of the key. So, for example, the *key of C major* is made up of the notes of the *C major scale*, C-D-E-F-G-A-B. If any note *other* than those appears in a piece that's written in the key of C, that note is said to be "outside the key." *Technical note:* "Outside the key" notes are referred to as *chromatic* tones. An *accidental* is a symbol—a sharp, flat, or natural—that indicates a departure from the notes of the key by the raising or lowering of one of those notes. So, in the key of C, any sharp or flat that indicates a black key is an *accidental*—because all black keys are "outside" the key of C; they are chromatic tones.

A point of interest: Some people mistakenly use the word *accidental* as a collective term to mean sharps, flats, and naturals. However, that's not technically correct. A sharp, flat, or natural is an accidental *only* when it's used to indicate a note outside the key, a chromatic tone. So, for example, in the key of E♭, which is based on the E♭ major scale, and which contains three flats (on B, E, and A), a flat on an E in *not* an accidental because the E♭ note is *in* the key; contrarily, a flat on D, or a natural on E, or a sharp on F, are considered accidentals because those tones are *outside* the key of E♭.

A technical point: You know that a half step is the distance from one key on the piano to the very next key, upward or downward, whether black or white. But there are two kinds of half steps; the two are equivalent in distance but they have different names. A half step consisting of two notes with the same letter name (for example, the half step from C to C-sharp) is called a *chromatic half step.* A half step consisting of consecutive letter names (such as C to D♭) is called a *diatonic half step.* Because major scales always are spelled with consecutive letters, with no letter repeated or skipped, any half step that occurs within a major scale (such as E to F in the C major scale) will, by definition, be a diatonic half step. Any chromatic half step that occurs in a piece of music will, by definition, involve a note outside the key, a so-called *chromatic* tone.

Another technical point: Although *diatonic* means "involving the notes belonging to the key (you're in)" and *chromatic* means "involving notes *not* belonging to the key (you're in)," the adjective *chromatic* sometimes is used to mean simply "moving by half steps," regardless of how the half steps are written in terms of letter names—whether with repeated or consecutive letter names. Also, note that whereas a major scale consists of seven consecutive letter names, the so-called *chromatic scale* is made up entirely of consecutive half steps and so includes *all* the keys, both black and white, on the piano. For example, an ascending chromatic scale starting from C is C-C♯-D-D♯-E, or C-D♭-D-E♭-E, and so on. So, the chromatic scale has a total of *twelve* different tones. In the chromatic scale the black keys can be spelled either as sharps or flats; that is, the half steps can be either chromatic half steps or diatonic half steps. By the way, the adjective *chromatic,* when referring to a musical instrument, means "capable of producing all the tones of the chromatic scale." So, whereas a *diatonic* harmonica produces only the seven tones of the major scale the harmonica is named after (a C harmonica, for example, produces the tones of the C major scale), a *chromatic* harmonica can produce all twelve tones of the chromatic scale.

READING AND PLAYING MUSIC IN VARIOUS KEYS

The next few examples give you a chance to read and play some famous classical melodies written in various keys, with sharps or flats indicated by the key signature rather than in the body of the music itself. The first example is Edward Elgar's famous "Pomp and Circumstance March No. 1," often played at graduation ceremonies. The key is B♭, so all Bs and Es are automatically flatted. This is notated in treble clef, so use your right hand.

Now try the same melody, but in a key that uses *sharps*—here, the key of A. As indicated by the key signature, all the Fs, Cs, and Gs are automatically sharped. This one's in bass clef, so use your left hand.

Next is the well-known "Minuet in G" from J. S. Bach's *Anna Magdalena Notebook.* You may know, from having seen the film *Mr. Holland's Opus,* that this was used as the basis of the 1965 pop hit "A Lover's Concerto." As the title suggests, we'll keep this one in the key of G, meaning that all Fs are automatically sharped. This is a treble clef example, so use your right hand.

Now we'll put the "Minuet in G" in bass clef and we'll transpose it to the key of A♭. (To *transpose* music means to move it to a different key.) The key of A♭ has a key signature of four flats—on B, E, A, and D; we automatically play those four pitches as flats. Use your left hand to play this example.

The final melody—Johann Strauss Jr's "On the Beautiful Blue Danube"—has a wide range, so we'll write this one on a grand staff. As usual, use your left hand for the bass-clef notes and your right for the treble-clef notes. Here it is in the key of E♭ (three flats), so all Bs, Es, and As are automatically flatted. Note that in the right-hand part, for each melody note you play *two* notes together, two notes at the exact same time. Notes stacked together vertically are always to be played at the same time.

ABOUT MINOR SCALES AND MINOR KEYS

We've spoken quite a bit about major scales and major keys—and most famous popular songs and classical pieces *are* in major keys. But some songs and pieces are in what's known as a *minor key.* You may have heard the phrase "in a minor key" used figuratively to mean "in a melancholy mood," and people often say that music in a minor key has a kind of sad sound. To get an idea of what music in a minor key sounds like, think of the Christmas carols "God Rest Ye Merry, Gentlemen" and "We Three Kings of Orient Are," or of the folk songs "House of the Rising Sun" and "Scarborough Fair."

Just as major keys are based on major scales, minor keys are derived from *minor scales.* What's a minor scale? Just as with a major scale, a minor scale is made up of seven consecutive letters, but the particular pattern of whole steps and half steps that make up a minor scale is different from that of a major scale.

If you play, on the piano keyboard, the white keys from A up to the next A, you get an A minor scale, A-B-C-D-E-F-G-A. You can hear right away that it doesn't have the familiar "do-re-me-fa-sol-la-ti-do" sound; instead, it has its own unique "minor scale" sound. Now, if you examine the whole steps and half steps that make up the A minor scale, you see that the pattern is "whole-half-whole-whole-half-whole-whole."

You may realize that the A minor scale uses the *exact same pitches* as the C major scale; the only difference is the starting point (C for the C major scale, but A for the A minor scale). Because the C major scale and the A minor scale use the same pitches, music based on those scales share the same key signature; that is, both the key of C major and A minor have a key signature of no sharps or flats. Also, because the C major scale and the A minor scale use the same pitches, the two scales are said to be *relative* to each other; that is, A minor is said to be the *relative minor* of C major, and C major is said to be the *relative major* of A minor.

You may also realize—again taking C major and A minor as an example—that the A note, the starting point of the relative minor scale, is the *sixth* degree of the relative major scale, the C major scale. You can count on you fingers from C up to A to confirm this. By extension, you realize that you can find the relative minor of any major scale simply by taking the notes of that scale but starting from the sixth degree. So, for example, F major and D minor are relative scales/keys, because D is the sixth degree of the F major scale. And because F major and D minor use the same seven tones in their scales, we know they share the same key signature, one flat.

We now know that the table of key signatures we displayed a bit earlier is incomplete; it shows only the *major* keys that are signified by the various key signatures. But each key signature can be used to represent either a major key *or* that key's relative minor key. We've already said that C major and A minor are relative to each other and share the same key signature, and that F major and D minor are relative to each other and share the same signature. Here is a table that shows *both* of the keys, major and minor, signified by each of the key signatures.

Sharp Keys

Key Signature	Major Key	Minor Key
1 sharp	G	E minor
2 sharps	D	B minor
3 sharps	A	F# minor
4 sharps	E	C# minor
5 sharps	B	G# minor
6 sharps	F#	D# minor
7 sharps	C#	A# minor

Flat Keys

Key Signature	Major Key	Minor Key
1 flat	F	D minor
2 flats	B♭	G minor
3 flats	E♭	C minor
4 flats	A♭	F minor
5 flats	D♭	B♭ minor
6 flats	G♭	E♭ minor
7 flats	C♭	A♭ minor

A point of interest: As key signatures add more sharps or flats, the sharps or flats are always added in the same order, in terms of how they're written on the staff, after the clef. For sharps, if you have a signature of *one* sharp (key of G or E minor), that sharp is placed on F. If you have a signature of *two* sharps, their order is F first, then C. For three sharps the order is F first, then C, then G. The complete order, for a signature of seven sharps is F, C, G, D, A, E, B. If you look back at the table of key signatures presented on the grand staff (p. 35), you'll see that this order is preserved from one key signature to the next. Students who want not only to read music but also to write music on paper memorize that order so that they can write key signatures quickly. A gimmick they sometimes use to remember the order is to think of the phrase "Fat Cows Get Dirty After Eating Brownies" or something similar. The order for placing flats on the staff is B, E, A, D, G, C, F. Again, a look back at the table of key signatures presented on the grand staff will confirm that the order is preserved from one signature to the next. Students want to write key signatures on paper can remember the order of flats by thinking of the work BEAD, followed by the phrase "German Can Factory" or something similar.

If two different keys share the same signature, how do you know which key the signature actually signifies? For example, if you see a signature of one sharp, how do you know whether the key is G major or E minor? One answer is that, for the sake of simply reading and playing the music, you don't need to know; you just play the notes written, remembering to sharp all the Fs. But if your curiosity demands to know, you can try to determine which note—either the G note or the E note, in this instance—feels like the tonic note; that is, which note feels like "home base." One or the other will probably feel like "home," or one or the other may serve as the ending note of the whole piece. That's probably the note that names the key.

READING AND PLAYING MUSIC IN MINOR KEYS

Play the example below with your right hand. The key signature is two flats, on B and E, which can signify either the key of B♭ major or G minor; here it's G minor. This is the famous melody from Mozart's Symphony No. 40 in G Minor, to which people have humorously applied the lyrics "Little Mozart is locked in the closet; let him out, let him out, let him out."

The next example is a melody that has been used numerous times by rock bands and in movies, video games, TV shows, and TV commercials. It's "In the Hall of the Mountain King," from Edvard Grieg's *Peer Gynt Suite.* If you don't recognize it by title, you will when you hear yourself play it. The original music begins in a low register, so we'll put this one in bass clef; play it with your left hand.

Here it's in the key of E minor, so all the Fs are played as F♯s. The example also includes some chromatic tones, tones outside the key; namely, A♯ and F♮. The sharp symbol in the third measure isn't technically necessary; it's there simply as a reminder or as a courtesy, because in the previous measure you play F♮ and sharps, flats, and naturals, as a rule, are in effect only in the measure in which they occur. "Reminder" sharps, flats, and naturals, such as this one, are called *courtesy accidentals*, whether they apply to notes outside the key or in the key.

A BIT MORE ABOUT MINOR SCALES

Although there is only one type of major scale, there are *three* different kinds of minor scales. The one we've been dealing with, which uses the same notes as its relative major scale, and on which key signatures are based, is known as the *natural minor scale*. All three types of minor scales are identical in their first five notes (degrees, steps); it's the sixth and seventh degrees that distinguish the various minor scales from one another.

Taking the *A natural minor scale* as an example, we have A-B-C-D-E-F-G-A. The so-called *A harmonic minor scale* is the same except that the seventh degree, G, is sharped, yielding A-B-C-D-E-F-G♯-A. And the so-called *A melodic minor scale* raises both the sixth and seventh degrees (A-B-C-D-E-F♯-G♯-A)— but only in the ascending form; when descending, the melodic minor is identical to the natural minor, with the sixth and seventh degrees unaltered: A-G-F-E-D-C-B-A. Of course, these definitions/exceptions concerning the sixth and seventh degrees apply to minor scales from *any* starting note, not just from A.

It's not important that you memorize this information or memorize the notes of the various minor scales. You can read music in minor keys even if you know nothing about the various forms of minor scales. What's important to realize is that the exact form of the minor scale employed by the composer—whether natural minor, harmonic minor, or melodic minor—has *no bearing* on the key signature; the key signature is *always* based on the *natural* minor scale—with any altered sixth and seventh scale degrees that may appear in the music indicated by means of accidentals (sharps, flats, or naturals before the individual note heads in question).

CHAPTER 5

ABOUT RHYTHM, PART 2

In Chapter 3 you played three different rhythmic figures: (1) *one* hit on a beat—for example, a quarter note in 4/4 time, which, in our musical sandwich, we said sounded like "bread," (2) *two* equal hits in a beat, which we said sounded like "cream cheese," and (3) *four* equal hits in a beat, which we said sounded like "peanut butter." We also sometimes had beats with no attack: either a silence or a continuation of a previously struck note; so, in a way, you played *four* different rhythmic possibilities. But what if a composer wishes to indicate that a beat should consist of *three* equally spaced notes?

ABOUT TRIPLETS

There's more than one way to indicate three equally spaced notes in written music, but for now we'll focus on a device known as a *triplet*; more about other methods later. First, continuing our food analogy, think of the three-syllable word "marmalade." Tap your foot in a steady rhythm, and for each tap say "mar-ma-lade." Make sure each syllable is the same duration. It might help to think of the phrase "ice cream cone" to get the sound of three equally spaced notes, but of course you wouldn't put an ice cream cone in a sandwich.

Now take a look at the example below, in which our sandwich, with three ingredients between the bread slices, is even more delicious. Try playing the example by simply tapping the rhythm or by playing it on the piano.

The "marmalade" beat above is a *triplet,* in this case, more specifically, an *eighth-note triplet,* which is three eighth notes, usually beamed together, with an italic numeral *3* centered above them. An eighth-note triplet indicates that *three* eighth notes are played in the time normally taken up by just *two* eighth notes—in other words, in the time of one beat. You can think of the numeral *3* above the notes as a kind of shorthand for the ratio *3:2*—meaning, *three* (of these notes) *in the* (normal) *time of two* (of these notes).

The next example demonstrates the use of an eighth-note triplet in a real song. You probably recognize from the lyrics that the example is the last phrase of "I've Been Working on the Railroad." Play it slowly, paying careful attention to the beat numbers under the lyrics.

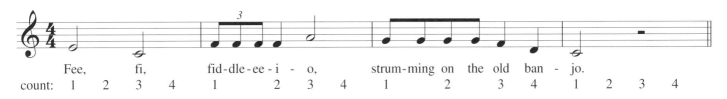

The next example mixes things up a bit. You play all the rhythmic figures you learned, including silences, in various orders. Keep the beats steady, and if necessary think of the four sandwich ingredients to remind you of the sound of each figure. In the first two measures you play varying rhythms on just one pitch; but in the final two measures you play varying rhythms on various pitches—just like in real-life music!

ABOUT PICKUPS

You know that the top number of the time signature tells you how many beats appear in each measure of the song or piece. But sometimes the first measure contains fewer beats than the number indicated. Take a look at the example below—the opening of the Christmas carol "O Come, All Ye Faithful."

The first measure above could begin with three beats of rest (as in the Mozart example—"Little Mozart is locked in the closet"—presented earlier); but it's common practice, in music whose first measure would begin with several beats of rest, to *omit* the rests and write only the notes that appear at the end of the measure. You can easily figure out which beat those notes start on by counting backward from the first bar line. In "O Come, All Ye Faithful," there is only one beat before the bar line, so it must be beat 4. An introductory note (or notes) like this is known as a *pickup*. And the opening shortened measure is known as a *pickup measure*. Sometimes, but not always, the *final* measure of a piece with a pickup also contains fewer beats than the number indicated by the time signature. The idea is to make it such that the pickup measure and the final measure together add up to the number of beats indicated by the time signature—so, in "O Come, All Ye Faithful," the final measure might contain only three beats. Added to the single beat of the pickup measure that makes four beats, as indicated by the 4/4 signature.

Below are two more Christmas carols that begin with pickups. Play them and see if you can identify them. The first is in 3/4 time with a one-beat pickup, so start counting on beat 3.

The next example is in 4/4 time and has a two-note pickup. Because they are eighth notes, they occur in one beat, so start counting from beat 4.

If you played the two examples correctly, you recognize them as "It Came Upon the Midnight Clear" and "The Twelve Days of Christmas," respectively.

ABOUT TIES

We've spoken about notes sustaining longer than one beat, such as a half note or a whole note in 2/4, 3/4, or 4/4 time. But what if you want a note to sustain for more than a whole measure? The example below, the opening of "By the Light of the Silvery Moon," demonstrates such a situation.

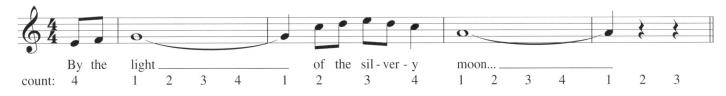

In the example above, the curved line connecting each whole note to the following quarter note is called a *tie*. A tie joins together two or more notes of the same pitch. When two notes are joined by a tie, you play the first of the two notes, but you allow it to sustain *for the combined value* of both notes. In this case, you play the whole note on beat 1 and allow it to sustain all the way through its own measure (four full beats) and you *continue to allow it to sustain through beat 1 of the following measure.* The lyrics of the song should help you get the feel of it.

Ties also can be used within a measure. The idea is the same: play the first of the two notes in question and allow it to sustain for the combined value of both notes. The next example is the opening of "She'll Be Comin' 'Round the Mountain." In the second and fourth full measures, play the half note on beat 1 and allow it to sustain through beat 3.

THE DOT

The next example is the same as the previous one (the opening of "She'll Be Comin' 'Round the Mountain"), but written in a slightly different way. Notice that in the second and fourth full measures, the two tied notes have been replaced by a single note with a little dot after it.

A *dot* (or, more specifically, an *augmentation dot*) is a shorthand way of writing a tie—but only if the second of the two tied notes is exactly half the length of the first. Looking at the first version of "She'll Be Comin' 'Round the Mountain" above, you see that the second tied note, a quarter note, is equal to exactly half the first note, a half note). Another way of stating this is to say that a dot adds to a note *half again as much* as the note's original value. So, if you add a dot to a half note (in 3/4 or 4/4 time), you get a total of three beats—two beats for the original value of the half note plus one more beat (half the value of the original note).

Although both versions of "She'll Be Comin' 'Round the Mountain" above are written properly, it's much more common for notators to use a dot than a tie when possible. So, the second version is probably how you'd see the song in a real-life situation.

Songs in 3/4 time that contain longish notes make great use of dotted half notes because each dotted half note, three beats, represents a full measure. Below are two examples of folk songs that use both dots and ties. Play them and see if you can identify them. In the first one—in the key of F in 3/4 time—remember not to strike the notes written in measures 4 and 8; instead, allow the previous note to continue to sustain.

The next example—in the key of D in 3/4 time—uses dots and ties, as well as a pickup. Again, remember not to strike the second note of each tied pair.

If you played the examples above correctly, you recognize them as "Down in the Valley" and "On Top of Old Smoky."

ABOUT TRICKY RHYTHMS

You can say that *easy* one-beat rhythmic combinations are the ones involving a pattern of repeating, equally spaced notes—such as two eighth notes in a beat (cream cheese) or four 16ths in a beat (peanut butter). The *tricky* rhythms, then, are the one-beat combinations in which you *don't hit* during *certain portions* of the beat, whether that portion is a rest or a continuation of a previously struck note. For example, tricky rhythms might include (1) a beat of two eighth notes in which you *don't* hit on the first eighth note, and (2) a beat of 16th notes in which you *don't* hit on the third 16th.

How can you learn the sounds of the tricky rhythms? As we mentioned earlier, you *shouldn't* try to play the rhythms by seeing how long each individual note lasts—a quarter of a beat, or a third a beat, or whatever the case may be. That's like trying to read text by looking at individual letters instead of full words. Rather, you try to memorize the sound of each of the various rhythmic figures that can occur in one beat. Then, when you read rhythmic notation, you simply count steady beats and apply the appropriate memorized rhythmic sound to each beat.

There are probably three or four different methods you can use for learning the sounds of the trickier one-beat rhythmic combinations. One is the method we've been using so far—thinking of a word or phrase that sounds like that rhythmic figure, as we used "cream cheese" for two eighth notes. For example, if you see a beat made up of an eighth note followed by two 16ths (meaning that you hit on the first, third, and fourth of the 16ths but not on the second), you can think of the word "strawberry." But when you say it, or think it, don't space the syllables evenly; instead, give more emphasis (a bit more time) to the first syllable: STRAW-ber-ry.

A second method is to find the figure in question in a famous song, then think of that song, or the appropriate beat of that song, to give you the sound of the figure. Again, taking an eighth followed by two 16ths as an examples, we find the figure near the beginning of "Skip to My Lou," as shown below.

A third method is what we like to call the "Bingo" method. You may remember that in the children's song "Bingo" ("There was a farmer who had a dog…"), when you spell out the dog's name, "B-I-N-G-O," you skip a letter (substituting silence) on each successive repetition of the song. So, the second time through, you sing "__-I-N-G-O," and the third time, "__-__-N-G-O," and so on. You can apply this idea for figuring out how various rhythms sound. For example, if you see a beat made up of an eighth rest followed by an eighth note, you can think of "cream cheese" but skip the "cream" portion, giving you "_____-cheese."

A final method involves a technique for playing easy (steady) rhythms that's presented in many books about reading music. It's similar to the method of using a word that sounds like the rhythm in question, but instead of using a real word, you say the number of the beat you're reading (1 or 2 or 3 or 4), plus a particular suffix. For example, if you see a series of steady *eighth notes* in, let's say, 2/4 time, instead of thinking "cream cheese, cream cheese," you think "1-and, 2-and." And if you see a series of steady *16th notes* in 2/4 time, instead of thinking "peanut butter, peanut butter," you think "1-e-&-a, 2-e-&-a" (pronounced "one-ee-and-uh, two-ee-and-uh"). And if you see a series of *eighth note triplets* in 2/4 time, instead of thinking "marmalade, marmalade," you think "1-trip-let, 2-trip-let." We haven't used this method simply because we believe that phrases like "cream cheese" and "peanut butter," whose sounds you're already familiar with, are more user friendly. However, if you need to figure out, on your own, the sound of a tricky one-beat rhythmic figure involving one, two, or three 16th notes, you can think of "1-e-&-a" and apply to it the "Bingo" method, in which you have no attack on certain of the syllables. For example, if you have a beat made up of a 16th rest followed by three 16th notes, you can say "__-e-&-a" to try to teach yourself the sound of that particular rhythmic combination. (In the same way, you can say "_____-nut but-ter" if you prefer a more user-friendly phrase.)

Now take a look at two of the rhythms discussed above—namely, (1) an eighth rest followed by an eighth note, and (2) an eighth note followed by two 16ths—in action in a real song. This is very song we happened to speak about above, "Bingo"!

TRICKY RHYTHMS INVOLVING EIGHTH NOTES

When you have a beat in 2/4, 3/4, or 4/4 time involving two eighth notes, you have a limited number of combinations of *hits* and *no hits*. You can have (1) "hit, hit" (which is simply two eighth notes, sounding like "cream cheese"), or (2) "hit, no hit" (which is a single attack on the beat, sounding similar to "bread"—if you say "bread" in a short, quick manner), or (3) "no hit, hit" (which we spoke of above and which sounds like "_____ cheese," or (4) "no hit, no hit" (which either is a full-beat rest or involves a continuation of a previously struck note).

Think about what happens when you tap your foot, one tap per beat, while you play music—your foot makes a "down-up" motion, moving *down* during the first half of the beat and *up* during the second. Of course, in rhythmic time, "down-up, down-up" corresponds to "cream cheese, cream cheese" or "1-and, 2-and." We said previously that the term *downbeat* is used to denote the first beat, as opposed to the subsequent beats, of a measure. This is true; but when speaking of individual beats, the word *downbeat* can also be used to denote the *first half* of the beat, the portion of the beat when your tapping foot moves down. And the term *upbeat* is used to denote the second half of the beat, when your foot moves up.

Looking again at the four possible combinations of hits and no hits described above, you see that for the first possibility you hit on both *downbeat and upbeat;* in the second you hit on *downbeat only;* in the third you hit on the *upbeat only;* and on the fourth you *don't hit at all*. You may realize that you're already quite familiar with *three* of those sounds—which basically correspond to "bread" (downbeat only), "cream cheese" (downbeat and upbeat), and *no attack*. And the remaining possibility, "_____ cheese" (upbeat only), isn't overly complex. So you may be asking yourself: "What's so tricky about reading rhythms with eighth notes?"

What makes the reading of rhythmic figures with eighth notes tricky is that certain written notations tend to obscure, visually, where beats begin and end; that is, you don't always see a note or rest at the beginning of each beat. For example, a long note will continue *beyond* its own beat, so no new symbol will appear at the beginning of the next beat. And the beats' starting and ending points can become even harder to discern when a long (or slightly long) note begins in the middle of a beat, or includes a dot that carries it beyond its own beat.

In the examples that follow, because it's sometimes hard to tell where beats involving eighth notes (that may or may not be struck) begin and end, we label each beat with one of the following letters: D, U, B, or N. *D* indicates that you hit on the *downbeat* only; this could apply either to a beat made up of an eighth note followed by an eighth rest or to a single quarter note. *U* indicates that you hit on the *upbeat* only; this could apply either to an eighth rest followed by an eighth note or to a continuation of a previous note on the downbeat and an eighth note on the upbeat. *B* indicates that you hit on *both* the downbeat and the upbeat (two eighth notes in a beat). *N* indicates that you hit on *neither* the downbeat nor the upbeat (either a silence or a continuation of a previous note).

The first example at the top of page 47 keeps things easy, with the beginning and end of each beat visually obvious. This example will get you accustomed to how the letter D, U, B, and N are being used—you can think to yourself *down, up, both, neither* for those letters, respectively. You can either play the notes on the piano or simply tap them. If you need to associate each beat with our "sandwich" syllables, you can think of "bread, cream cheese, bred, *rest* | cream cheese, _____ cheese, bread, bred" (with "bread" intentionally misspelled as "bred" to show that the note in question is shortened; that is, it's held for half the beat rather than for the full beat).

The next example includes ties. But the beginnings and ends of the beats are still clearly seen. Play this or tap it.

The next example is the same as the one above, but in measure 1, as is customary, a dot is used instead of a tie. This causes there to be no note written at the beginning of beat 2, thus visually obscuring the beginning of that beat.

In the second measure of the example above, instead of tying the second half of beat 1 to the first half of beat 2, we write, as is generally customary, a quarter note beginning at the second half of beat 1. This visually obscures the beginning of beat 2, because no new note is written there. But by comparing the example above to the one that precedes it, you can see that they are indeed played the same, and you can see that—through an understanding of D, U, B, and N—it's possible to determine where each beat begins, even when no new notes are written at those beats' starting points.

A technical point: In measure 2 of the previous example, you see a quarter note beginning in the middle of a beat. This is an example of a rhythmic device known as *syncopation.* Usually, downbeats are emphasized (or stressed) more than upbeats. So foot tapping, for example, is more like "DOWN-up, DOWN-up" than "down-UP, down-UP." In syncopation, that stress pattern is temporarily altered.

So, whenever you have a stress where you don't expect it, or *don't* have a stress where you *do* expect it, that's syncopation. For example, composer Stephen Foster syncopated the rhythm of the word *river* when he wrote "Way down upon the Swanee Ri-VER."

The next few examples are from songs whose notation sometimes obscures the beginnings of beats. Try playing them, paying attention to the letters D, U, B, and N written above the notes. In the first example, the dotted quarter notes on beat 1 of each measure visually obscure beat 2. But the letter U at the beginning of each beat 2 helps you see the beat—and reminds you to hit only on the upbeat half of the beat, with the downbeat half a continuation of beat 1's dotted quarter note.

The next example employs, at the beginning of the third full measure, an example of syncopation: a stressed note (here, a dotted quarter note) beginning on the unstressed portion of the beat, as in the Stephen Foster example above. If you examine the beats in question (first half of measure 3) you see that *beat 1* contains two hits—an eighth note on the first half of the beat and a (syncopated) dotted quarter note that begins on the second half; thus, beat 1 is indicated as B, for *both,* meaning that you hit on *both* halves of the beat. *Beat 2* contains no hits, because the dotted quarter note beginning at the second half of beat 1 lasts for a total of one and a half beats and thus continues to ring throughout all of beat 2; thus, the indication N, meaning that *neither* half of beat 2 gets struck.

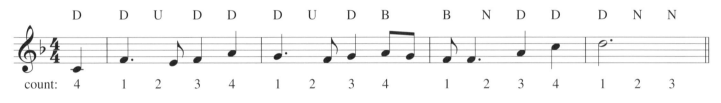

If you played the two examples above correctly, you recognize them as "America, the Beautiful" and "Auld Lang Syne," respectively.

TRICKY RHYTHMS INVOLVING 16TH NOTES

We said earlier that tricky rhythmic figures involving 16th notes are those one-beat combinations in which you hit only *some* of four 16ths that make up the beat rather than all four of them. And we talked about how you can learn the sounds of these combinations by thinking of a word that sounds like the figure in question, as we illustrated with the word *strawberry* for the figure of an eighth followed by two 16ths, or by finding an example of the figure in a famous song, as we demonstrated the same figure with the lyrics "skip to my" in the song "Skip to My Lou." We also said you could determine how some 16th-note figures sound by combining the "1-e-&-a" method with what we called the "Bingo" method, in which you skip certain syllables, as desired.

In this section we look at one-beat 16th-note figures commonly seen, and you learn how they sound by means of one or another of the methods mentioned above. But first, an additional factor is worthy of note. You already learned about the figure that sounds like the word *strawberry.* In that figure you hit on the first, third, and fourth 16th notes of the beat, but not on the second. When we described that figure, we called it an eighth note followed by two 16ths. But look at two beats of the example that follows. In the second beat, as in the first, you hit on all the 16ths except the second one; however, whereas in the first beat you sustain the first note for half the beat, the entire downbeat portion of the beat, in the second beat you cut that first note short, to allow for the silence indicated by the 16th rest.

count: 1   2

The important point is that whether you see the first version of the figure *or* the second, think of *your same memorized sound* when you read/play it (whether it's a word, like *strawberry,* or—if you've gone beyond relying on words—simply the musical sound of the figure itself). You simply make a slight adjustment to the length of the first note when you play it. For all the one-beat 16th-note combinations we look at in this section, be aware that they exist in more than one form; that is, certain notes in the figure may be either sustained or cut short, as in the "strawberry" example we just looked at. But because composers generally allow notes to sustain rather than cut them short, we'll use the "sustain" versions in our demonstrations; simply remember to shorten certain notes in performance if shorter notes are indicated.

Another common 16th-note figure is kind of the reverse of the one discussed above; it's two 16ths followed by an eighth. So, you hit on the first, second, and third 16ths, but not the fourth. It sounds kind of like the word "cantaloupe" or "mayonnaise." The example below, a few bars from the middle of "This Old Man," demonstrates the figure in action (second beat of measure 3).

In another common figure involving 16th notes, you hit on the first and fourth 16ths, but not on the second or third. The figure is usually written as a dotted-eighth note beamed together with a 16th note. (Note that, according to the rules of augmentation dots, a dotted-eighth note is equivalent in length to an eighth plus a 16th, or three-quarters of a beat in 2/4, 3/4, and 4/4 time.) The example below, the opening of "Battle Hymn of the Republic," demonstrates the sound of the figure.

The figure can also be heard in such songs as "Clementine," "Joy to the World," "Kumbaya," "O Christmas Tree," and "Here Comes the Bride." Sing these out loud or in your mind and see if you can tell which beats would be notated as a dotted quarter and a 16th.

Another common figure is an eighth rest followed by two 16th notes. You can learn the sound of this pattern by noting its use in the middle of this passage from Handel's famous "Hallelujah Chorus" from *Messiah*. (See page 50.) By the way, the curved line above the first two notes of the last measure is a *slur*. In vocal music it's used to show that notes slurred together, encompassed by the slur, are sung on the same syllable; in instrumental music it shows that the slurred notes are to be played smoothly, with no separation between them.

Below is an exercise that allows you to play the 16th-note figures you learned. You can play it on the piano or simply tap it out. Count only *beats*—by tapping your foot, or saying the beat numbers out loud, or by merely feeling the beats in the back of your mind. Look at beats 3 and 4 of measure 3. Here a dotted quarter note on beat 3 visually obscures the beginning of beat 4. But by examination you see that beat 4 consists of hits on only the third and fourth 16th notes of the beat, so think of the sound you learned in the *Messiah* example to play this beat; remember, though, that in the first half of the beat you have a continuation of the previous note's sound rather than a silence.

MORE 16TH-NOTE FIGURES

In addition to the 16th-note figures we describe above, there are seven others you may run across. But for these we won't give you words that sound like them or famous songs that contain them. Instead, use the "1-e-&-a" technique combined with the "Bingo" method to sound out each figure. The chart below illustrates this for the seven additional figures; the music has no time signature because we're showing seven separate examples, not seven measures. Say "1-e-&-a" out loud, but *omit* the appropriate syllable or syllables; the syllables indicated in parentheses are the ones you *don't* say. Repeat each figure out loud, over and over; pay attention to each resulting sound and memorize it. The last example below includes a dotted-eighth rest, equivalent in length to an eighth rest plus a 16th rest. This demonstrates that dots may be added to rests as well as to notes. Just as with notes, a dot adds to a rest *half again as much* as the duration of the original rest.

The example below—the opening of Scott Joplin's "The Entertainer," which was famously used as the theme music for the 1973 film *The Sting*—gives you a chance to see some of these trickier 16th-note figures in action.

CHAPTER 6
ABOUT METER

As you know, the time signature of a piece tells you how many beats are in a measure, which note value is equivalent to one beat, and which beats of each measure are stressed or unstressed. For example, in 4/4 time there are *four* beats in a measure, the *quarter note* represents the beat, and the *first* beat of each measure is stressed (with a *secondary* stress on beat 3). The *meter* of a piece of music can be defined as the number of beats that are grouped together into measures and the relative stresses of those beats. So, the word *meter* means pretty much the same thing as the term *time signature.* In fact, a time signature is sometimes called a "meter signature."

Time signatures are sometimes categorized by how they function; that is, certain time signatures considered collectively are given a particular category name (or heading)—and these category names include the term *meter* rather than the term *time signature.*

One way time signatures are grouped together, or classified, is in terms of how many beats they contain in each measure. For example, any time signature with a 2 as the top number (such as 2/4, 2/2, and 2/8) has *two* beats per measure and is referred to as *duple meter.* Likewise, any time signature with 3 as the top number (such as 3/4, 3/2, and 3/8) has *three* beats per measure and is referred to as *triple meter.* Similarly, a signature with 4 as the top number is *quadruple meter,* a signature with 5 as the top number (signifying five beats per measure) is *quintuple meter,* and so on. But duple, triple, and quadruple meters are by far the most common meters.

The other way time signatures are categorized is by how their individual beats naturally divide themselves; that is, do they naturally divide themselves into *two* equal parts, as in "TWIN-kle, TWIN-kle, LIT-tle STAR," or into *three* equal parts, as in "FOL-low the YEL-low brick ROAD," with the capitalized syllables representing the beginnings of beats. If the beats naturally divide themselves into two parts, the meter is said to be a *simple meter*, regardless of how many beats are in each measure and regardless of which note value represents the beat. All the example you've played so far have been in simple meters. But if the beats naturally divide themselves into *three* equal parts, again regardless of how many beats are in each measure and regardless of which note value represents the beat, the meter is said to be a *compound meter.* Later in this chapter we take a look at some music in compound meters.

ABOUT CUT TIME (2/2 TIME)

So far, in all the music you've played, the quarter note was the note value that represented the beat (as in 2/4, 3/4, and 4/4 time). But sometimes another note value, such as a half note or an eighth note, is chosen to represent the beat. A common time signature (meter) in which the *half* note receives the beat is 2/2 time—that is, two beats per measure (as indicated by the time signature's *top* number), with the half note representing the beat (as indicated by the time signature's *bottom* number), and with beat 1 stressed (and beat 2 unstressed).

Below is how the chorus of "Jingle Bells" looks if written in 2/4 time; that is, if the notator chose the quarter note to represent the beat and chose to group the beats in twos.

Now compare that to the exact same melody below, but here written in 2/2 time; that is, with the *half note* representing one beat and the beats grouped in twos.

The important point is that although the two examples above *look* different, they are counted and played *in exactly the same way.* If you wonder which of the two versions is the proper notation, the answer is that each one is correct. It's the notator's choice as to which note value represents the beat and how the beats are grouped together into measures. The decision is based on what he thinks will be easiest for musicians to read and understand. Notator A might feel that the former version is easiest, but Notator B might feel that it's the latter. That's why, in the real world, you may see the same song notated in more than one way in various publications.

By comparing the two examples above, you see that each one-beat sound you learned in meters with a *quarter note* beat looks different when written in a meter with a *half note beat.* For example, in beat 1 of the first measure you have the sound of two hits in one beat, what we called the "cream cheese" sound in our food analogy; but whereas in 2/4 time the sound is written as two *eighth* notes, in 2/2 time that same sound is written as two *quarter* notes. And also take, as another example, the second half of the third measure (where the lyric is "all the"); whereas in 2/4 time that one-beat sound is written as a dotted eighth followed by a 16th, in 2/2 time that same sound becomes a dotted quarter followed by an eighth.

For each common one-beat rhythmic figure in 2/4 time, or in any meter in which the quarter note represents the beat, there is a corresponding rhythmic figure—*that sounds exactly the same*—in 2/2 time, or in any meter in which the half note represents the beat. The chart given here shows, side by side, how the 15 rhythmic figures you learned look when written in meters with a quarter note beat and in meters with a half note beat.

A technical point: 2/2 time is generally referred to as *cut time,* and its signature is usually written not as 2/2, but with a symbol that looks kind of like a capital *C* with a vertical line through it. It's also worth mentioning that 4/4 time is often referred to as *common time*— after all, it is probably is the most common time signature and is *sometimes* indicated not by 4/4 but by the same C-shaped symbol but *without* a vertical line through it.

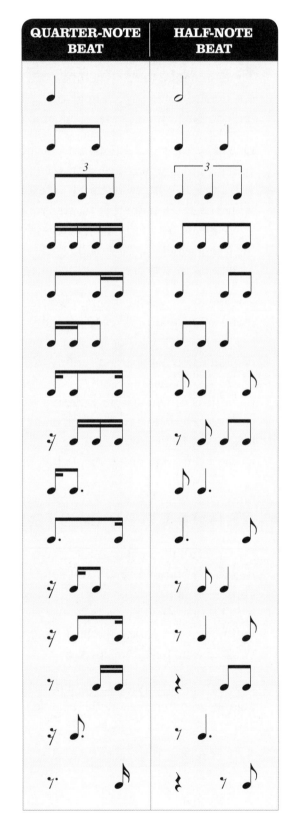

A point of interest: Some people believe that when the C-shaped symbol is used to indicate 4/4 time, it's a letter *C,* standing for the word *common.* But the symbol is actually a stylized *semicircle* rather than a stylized capital *C.* You see, in centuries past, musicians divided time signatures into two groups: what they called *perfect time* and *imperfect time.* If the number of beats in a measure was *three,* the time signature was indicated by a full circle and the meter was called *perfect*—because the Christian doctrine of the Holy Trinity defines God as *three* persons: the Father, the Son, and the Holy Spirit. But if the number of beats in a measure was two or four (which don't match the number of the Holy Trinity), the meter was called *imperfect,* and the time signature was indicated by a semicircle (the left half of a circle). So, the C-looking symbols used for today's common time and cut-time signatures are holdovers from the old semicircle; it's not really a letter C.

Below is a song for you to play that's often notated in cut time (2/2/ time)—George M. Cohan's "Give My Regards to Broadway." Pay attention to the beat numbers below the lyrics; these remind you that, because you are in cut time, the *half note* receive the beat. Also, because this is your first time reading/playing a song in cut time (in which the rhythmic notation you're accustomed to seeing is now doubled), we've indicated, below the beat numbers, the letters D, U, B, and N to remind you whether, for each beat, you should hit on the *downbeat* portion only (D), the *upbeat* portion only (U), *both* the downbeat and upbeat portions (B), or neither the downbeat nor the upbeat portions (N).

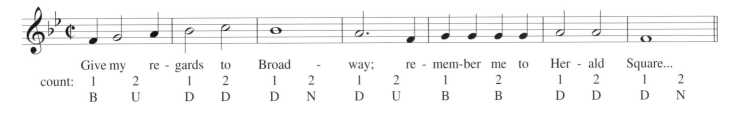

A technical point: Some people believe that cut time means to play the music twice as fast as normal. If you look above at "Give My Regards to Broadway" and you imagine that the time signature is 4/4 and you play it at double speed, you'll get something similar to our actual cut-time version. However, the *feel* will be wrong; that is, instead of a feel of two moderate-tempo beats per measure, you'll end up with a feel of four fast-tempo beats per measure. So, when reading/playing in cut time, never think about playing at double speed. Simply remember that it's the half note that represents the beat, and realize that the appearance of all the rhythmic figures you memorized will be different, owing to the doubling of the note values.

ABOUT COMPOUND TIME

We mentioned previously that in compound time, the beats naturally divide themselves in thirds rather than halves, as illustrated by the phrase FOL-low the YEL-low brick ROAD (with the capitalized syllables indicating the beginnings of beats). Simple time (in which beats naturally divide themselves in halves) is easier to notate than is compound time because in simple time, for each note value, there exists *another* note value that's half its length. For example, a half note can divide into two quarter notes, a quarter can divide into two eighths, an eighth can divide into two 16ths, and so on. By the way, if we keep on dividing into smaller units, we can produce 32nd notes (indicated with three flags or beams), 64th notes (indicated with four flags or beams), and so on—though notes smaller than 32nds are rarely used. On top of that, any note value that can be divided in half (which is any value mentioned above in this paragraph) can be used as the bottom number of a time signature, to indicate that that value represents the beat.

But in compound time, in which notes naturally divide themselves into thirds, it's a *dotted* note that represents a beat. That's because, for example, a *dotted quarter note* can be divided into *three eighth notes.* And, in fact, in compound time, the dotted quarter note *is* the unit that most frequently represents the beat. The problem, though, is that the bottom number of a time signature is simply a numeral (usually 2, 4, or 8)—and this numeral always indicates what kind of *undotted* note represents the beat.

So, if a notator wishes to indicate, say, two beats per measure, with each beat consisting of three equal parts, he must write three eighth notes for beat 1, plus another three eighth notes for beat 2, for a total of *six eighth notes.* And so, for his time signature, he's forced to write 6/8—not because he has six eighth-note beats; he actually has two dotted-quarter-note beats, but because 6/8 is the closest signature there is to what he's writing; that is, a total of six eighth notes in each measure (at least it adds up correctly).

But take a look at the example below, which shows that 6/8 time, technically speaking, is *not* compound duple time (*two* beats per measure, with the beats dividing themselves into *thirds*); rather, it's *simple sextuple time* (*six* beats per measure, with the beats dividing themselves into *halves*).

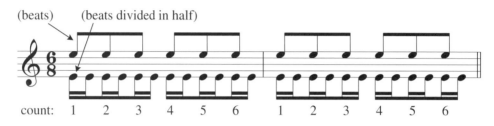

But even though *technically* 6/8 time is simple sextuple, far more often it's used to indicate compound duple, as shown below. Note that in this example we add a *tempo heading* (a word or phrase placed at the beginning of a composition that tells you how fast or slow the beat is), and that the heading includes the phrase "in 2." This instruction makes it clear that there are two beats per measure—and so it's the *dotted quarter* (not the eighth) that represents the beat, and there are *two* beats per measure; in other words, *compound duple* meter.

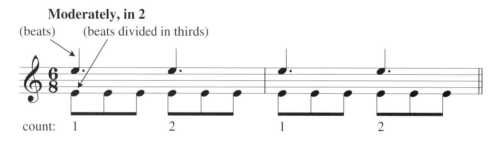

Note that if the phrase "in 2" doesn't appear as part of the tempo heading of a piece in 6/8 time, it's still very likely that it's the dotted quarter note, not the eighth note, that's receiving the beat. However, if the tempo is very slow, it's quite possible that the piece consists of six eighth-note beats per measure (simple sextuple time).

Now take a look at 6/8 time, the compound duple version of it, in action in a real song—"For He's a Jolly Good Fellow." The beat numbers under the lyrics emphasize the fact that the song has just two beats per measure, not six. Because you're familiar with the song, you know how the various rhythms of the individual beats of the song should sound. But if you want to read/play a piece in 6/8 time that you're *not* already familiar with, you need to know how the various common one-beat rhythmic combinations of 6/8 time sound.

You already know the sound of three equal notes in a beat, as demonstrated by the lyrics "jol-ly good" in the song above—it's the same as the sound of an eighth-note triplet in 2/4 time; in other words, the sound of "ice cream cone" or "mar-ma-lade," which you've already learned. And you know the sound of a single hit on a beat (occurring in the song above on the first syllable of the word "fel-low"—and notated as a dotted-quarter note). The other common one-beat rhythmic combinations in 6/8 time— there are five of them—result from hitting just two, or one, of the three eighth notes that make up the beat rather than all three.

The chart below illustrates this for the five additional figures. The music has no time signature because we're showing five separate one-beat examples, not five measures. Whereas the phrase "1-e-&-a" is commonly used for counting out a beat of 16th notes in simple meters, no standard phrase exists for counting out beats of three eighth notes in compound time. But some people have used "1-&-ah, 2-&-ah" (which, as you realize, sounds the same as "ice cream cone, ice cream cone"). To teach yourself the sound of each of these five figures, say "1-&-ah" out loud, but *omit* the appropriate syllable or syllables (as before, the syllables indicated in parentheses in the examples below are the ones you *don't* say). Just as you did when learning 16th-note figures in simple time, repeat each figure, out loud, over and over, paying attention to each resulting sound. By the way, the last example begins with a quarter rest, but it could have been written as two eighth rests instead (because one quarter rest equals two eighth rests). And note that a beat of silence in 6/8 time is usually written as a dotted-quarter rest, though it's sometimes written as a quarter rest followed by an eighth rest.

Observe that some of the five sounds include a quarter note in their notation. Take, for example, the first figure: an eighth note followed by a quarter, which has the sound of hitting on the first two eighth notes of the beat but not on the third. In actual practice, the figure could appear exactly like that, or it might be written as two eighth notes followed by an eighth rest, if the composer wishes to make the second note short. The important point is that the sound of each of these versions is basically the same; that is, you hit and don't hit in exactly the same places. So keep in mind that in performance—just as with the various one-beat 16th-note figures you learned for simple meters—you sometimes may need to make a slight adjustment to your memorized sound by playing one of the notes in a shortened fashion, if that's what the composer indicated.

Below are two well-known songs in 6/8 time. Play them counting two beats per measure, not six. Each song relies heavily on the rhythmic figure in which you hit on the first and third eighth notes of the beat, the sound represented by the lyrics "he's a" in "For He's a Jolly Good Fellow" above. First play this children's classic.

Now play this Christmas classic.

If you played the two songs above correctly, you recognize them as "Eency, Weency Spider" and "I Saw Three Ships," respectively.

Compound duple time (in other words, 6/8 time) is the most commonly used compound time, but pieces also are written in *compound triple* (in other words, 9/8 time, with *three* dotted-quarter-note beats per measure) and *compound quadruple* (12/8 time, with *four* dotted-quarter-note beats per measure). For example, the song below, written in 12/8 time, is in compound quadruple meter.

A word about 3/8 time: You may wonder whether music in 3/8 time (three eighth notes per measure) is *compound* time (one dotted quarter note beat per measure) or *simple* time (three eighth note beats per measure). It's rare for a composer to write just one beat per measure. That's why although we speak of *duple* time (two beats per measure), *triple* time (three beats), and so on, we don't speak of what might be called "single time." So, if a composer wants the dotted quarter to represent the beat, he'd be much more likely to write in 6/8 than in 3/8, thus grouping the beats in twos rather than in ones. Consequently, if you see 3/8 time, it's most likely simple triple time, three eighth-note beats per measure. However, today's notators rarely use 3/8 time, in which eighth notes indicate beats and 16ths indicate half beats; instead, to write music in simple triple time, they much prefer 3/4 time, with quarters notes indicating beats and eighth notes indicating half beats. But in previous centuries, back in the time of Bach or Mozart, simple triple time often *was* written in 3/8 time. So, if you encounter a piece from back then written in 3/8 time, allow each eighth note to receive a beat. In sight reading such a piece, you may find it easier to mentally double all the values and pretend that you're reading in 3/4 instead of 3/8.

Let's say a composer is writing in compound time, for example 6/8 time, and he wants notes that are shorter than eighth notes; in other words, what if he wants more than just three notes in a beat. Although in compound time the dotted-quarter-note beat naturally divides itself in thirds (in the form of three eighth notes), each individual eighth, if divided into smaller values, divides itself in *halves*. So, instead of writing three eighth notes in a beat, a composer—desiring more notes in a beat—might write six 16th notes, as shown in the second measure of the example below.

Note, in the second measure above, that 16th notes in compound time can be beamed in groups of *two* by means of breaks in their 16th beams, to emphasize the fact that three eighth notes make up the beat, or in groups of *six*, to emphasize the fact that the six notes make up a single beat. That's the notator's choice, but beaming in six is more common. To teach yourself the sound of six 16ths as a single beat of compound time, you can think of a phrase that has the same accentuation as those notes; namely, stressed-unstressed, stressed-unstressed, stressed-unstressed—for example, the phrase "little bitty kitty," or anything similar that you might prefer. Then, to teach yourself the sounds of various permutations of 16th notes in compound time, you can apply the "Bingo" method to the "little bitty kitty" phrase, omitting the appropriate syllables. The example below illustrates this process for a few common permutations.

The example below gives you a chance to read/play a song in compound time that includes 16th notes.

If you played the example above correctly, you recognize it as "Home on the Range."

Note that a piece of music needn't remain in one meter throughout. A composer might write several bars of 4/4, and then switch to 3/4 for one or more measures. The portion of the well-known song "The Twelve Days of Christmas" shown below illustrates this concept.

ABOUT TUPLETS

As you know, in a meter like 2/4, 3/4, or 4/4, an eighth-note triplet indicates three notes of equal duration, written as eighth notes with an italic *3* above them, to be played in the time of one beat (or, to say it another way, in the time of *two* eighth notes). But what if you want more than three notes of equal duration to be played in one beat. Well, for four equal notes in a beat you simply write four 16th notes, and for eight equal notes in a beat you write eight 32nd notes. But what if you want five, or six, seven, or nine equal notes in a beat?

All these so-called *odd groupings* can be indicated in a fashion similar to that of the eighth-note triplet: that is, by writing the number of notes desired with an italic numeral above (or sometimes below) them. The notes in question are either beamed together or indicated by means of a horizontal bracket surrounding the numeral. The numeral, in effect, says: Play the number of notes indicated in the time normally taken by the number of notes of this time value that *would* normally fit in one beat.

For example, if, in 4/4 time, you see five 16th notes with an italic *5* above them, this tells you to play the five 16th (equally spaced) in the time normally taken by *four* 16ths (in other words, in the time of *one beat*). Similarly, seven 16th notes with an italic *7* above them tells you to play the seven 16ths in the time four 16ths (one beat)—because *four* 16ths is what normally fits in one beat.

Any odd grouping indicated by means of a numeral above notes is given the generic term *tuplet.* The specific tuplets includes the *triplet* (three notes in the time of two), the *quintuplet* (five notes in the time of four), the *sextuplet* (six notes in the time of four), the *septuplet* (*seven* notes in the time of four), and so on.

For nine equal notes (a *nontuplet*) in, say, 4/4 time, instead of writing nine *16ths* (with an italic *9* above), we write nine *32nds.* The idea is that, generally speaking, for all tuplets, if you were to ignore the italic numeral above, the number of notes in the tuplet is *too large* for the beat (as you saw with the eighth note triplet, where *three* eighth notes was *too many* for one beat). But the note value chosen for a tuplet is always the *smallest* value that can be used but that still allows the total number of tuplet notes to be *too large* for the beat. So, again calling on your inner mathematician, you see that because the number of 32nd notes that *normally* fit in a beat of, say, 4/4 is *eight,* then *nine 32nds* would be too many. So, in other words, 32nds do the job of making the tuplet too big for the beat if you disregard the numeral above (and so it would be incorrect to use 16ths in this case).

How do we count out odd groupings such as five or seven notes in a beat of 4/4 time? Unfortunately, there are no particular words or phrases commonly relied upon that sound like these rhythms. And there are no commonly used "1-e-&-a" type tricks for them either. But if you tap your foot in a slow or moderate but steady beat, then for each beat you can count (out loud if you like) "one-two-three-four-five" for a quintuplet, or "one-two-three-four-five-six" for a sextuplet, and so on. This should give you the sounds of the various tuplet figures. The example below lets you try out some of these rhythms. Play them on the piano or simply tap them.

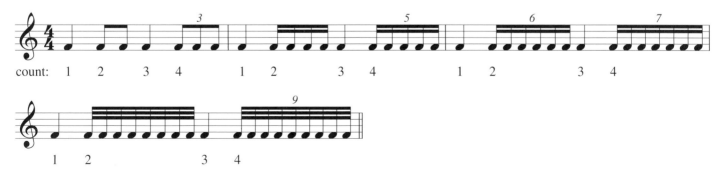

Note that in the example above we don't need tuplets for the groups of four or eight equal notes—because quarter notes can be divided in four 16ths and into eight 32nds. In fact, in simple time (such as 2/4, 3/4, and 4/4), you never need tuplets for a number of equal notes that can be found in the series 2, 4, 8, 16, 32… because quarter notes can be divided into these many equal parts simply by means of smaller note values (two eighths, four 16ths, eight 32nds, and so on).

However, in compound time, where a dotted note receives the beat, we have a different situation. Because a dotted note divides itself into *three* parts, and then because those smaller parts divide themselves in *halves* (and again and again in halves as they continue to divide), in compound time you never need tuplets for a number of equal notes that can be found in the series 3, 6, 12, 24… because dotted quarter notes can be divided into these many equal parts simply by means of smaller note values (three eighths, six 16ths, twelve 32nds, and so on). The example below illustrates this concept. It also illustrates a *quadruplet* (four-note odd grouping) and an *octuplet* (eight-note odd grouping). Play the example on the piano or tap it.

You may notice in the example above that we don't divide the dotted-quarter-note beat into *two* equal parts. However, this rhythm is indeed a possibility, and it can be notated with smaller note values, as in beat 2 of measure 1 below, which indicates an attack on the beat and another attack halfway through the beat. Each attack lasts for the equivalent of three 16ths' worth of time.

Another way to write two equal attacks in a beat of compound time is as a tuplet—specifically, a *duplet* (two equal notes in the time of three). On beat 2 of measure 2 above, you see this as a *quarter-note duplet*, which also demonstrates the use of a horizontal bracket to indicate the notes in question. This notation, preferred by some notation experts, follows the general rule that if you were to remove the tuplet numeral, you'd be left with *too much music for the beat.* But on beat 2 of measure 3 above, you see this same rhythm notated as an *eighth-note duplet*. This notation, preferred by other notation experts, follows the general rule that for a duplet you play two notes in the time normally taken by three *of that same time value.*

Which notation is correct? Both are widely used, but we prefer the *quarter-note* duplet because it seems more consistent with the notation of other compound time tuplets. For example, if *four eighth notes* (with a *4* above) indicate one beat in, say, 6/8 time, it seems logical that *two quarters notes* (with a *2* above) should equal that same amount of time. After all, generally speaking, two quarters are equivalent to four eighth notes.

ABOUT THE QUARTER-NOTE TRIPLET

All the tuplets we've discussed so far, whether in simple time or compound time, take up the time of one beat. But one particular tuplet found in simple time, the *quarter-note triplet,* takes the time of *two* beats. To say it another way, it consists of the three equally spaced notes in the time of two beats, as illustrated in the example below.

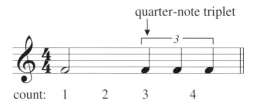

How does this tricky looking rhythm sound? We can illustrate it by mentioning famous songs that use it, but you can also count it out by mentally converting it to two *one-beat* figures. More on that later.

Using the "famous song" method, we can point out that particular words in the titles of certain standards, when those words are sung in the lyrics of the song, are, indeed, sung as quarter-note triplets. (Note that in the following sentences, the bold syllables represent quarter-note triplets.) For example, Fats Domino famously sang that he found his thrill on "**Blue-ber-ry** Hill." And Ira Gershwin, writing with brother George and others, pointed out that what you might read in the Bible "**ain't nec-es-sar-i-ly** so" (two consecutive quarter-note triplets). And lyricist Howard Dietz, writing with composer Arthur Schwartz, said that what filled him with desire was "**you and the night and the** music" (again, two consecutive quarter-note triplets).

Another way to count out a quarter-note triplet, as we said, is by mentally converting the two-beat figure into two one-beat figures. The example below shows how this is done. Focusing on the second half of each measure, note that measure 1 contains a quarter-note triplet. Measure 2 has the same rhythm as measure 1, but the quarter-note triplet has been rewritten as two *eighth-note triplets.* By examination, you see that in each case you have three equal attacks in two beats; this confirms that the rhythms are indeed the same. Of course, you're accustomed to seeing tuplets (at least, so far in this book) as a group of *equal notes* that match in number the tuplet numeral above. But the individual notes of a tuplet, in actual practice, might be tied, or dotted, or omitted, and so on, sometimes causing the notes that make up the tuplet *not* to be all of the same duration. Also by examination you see that measure 3 below contains the same rhythm as measure 1, including three equal attacks in two beats. And, because you studied the various combinations of eighth notes in one beat of compound time, the rhythm of measure 3 is one you already know! Simply think of this rhythm when you see a quarter-note triplet in simple time, or feel free to employ the "famous song" approach described above.

A Notation Dilemma?: Let's say a piece contains numerous beats that are divided in halves (or quarters) and *also* contains numerous beats that are divided in thirds. Should the notator write the piece in *simple* time, with triplets for the odd groupings (as in measure 1 below), or *compound* time, with duplets and quadruplets for the odd groupings (as in measure 2 below, which, as you see by examination, has the same rhythm as measure 1)? Is one correct and one incorrect?

Usually, in a piece in which some beats are divided into halves and others into thirds, one or the other division will sound natural and normal while the other sounds off-kilter and odd (hence the phrase "odd grouping"). If a division of the beat into halves sounds normal, simple meter is used; but if a division of the beat into halves sounds odd, with a division into thirds sounding normal, compound time is used. However, all things being equal (with neither a division of the beat into *halves* sounding particularly normal or odd, nor a division of the beat into *thirds* sounding particularly normal or odd), the notator is free to use *either* simple or compound time. His choice usually will be based on what he feels, and arbitrarily decides, will be easier for the reader to understand and play.

By the way, along the same lines, a notator might also arbitrarily decide *how many beats* should be contained in each measure—based mostly on what he thinks will properly convey the feeling of the song, but sometimes simply based on what he thinks will be easiest for people to read. For example, in a previous chapter, we notated "The Farmer in the Dell" in 12/8 time (four beats per measure); but a different notator might just as easily choose 6/8 time (two beats per measure).

CHAPTER 7

SPECIAL WORDS AND SYMBOLS

In previous chapters you studied the two most important aspects of reading music: reading pitch and reading rhythm. But music notation often provides additional information concerning *how* you play the music; that is, do you play it fast or slow, loud or soft, smoothly or choppily? Questions concerning the production of successive notes (for example, are they connected smoothly or in a detached manner?) fall under the heading of *articulation*. Questions concerning how fast and how loudly you play the music fall under the heading of *expression*. In addition, music notation often contains instructions concerning repeats (that is, indications that certain measures or passages are to be played more than once), and this is a concern of musical *form*. And the addition of decorative embellishments to notes is known as *ornamentation*. In this chapter, we look at special words and symbols that indicate the particulars of musical articulation, expression, form, and ornamentation—as well as at a few miscellaneous symbols concerning pitch and rhythm.

ARTICULATION

About staccato: Sometimes successive notes in a piece are played smoothly and sometimes in a detached manner. Think of the low, ominous theme to the movie *Jaws*. You know, "Bum-bum-bum-bum…" You can hear that the notes are played in a detached manner, or, to use musical terminology, the notes are played *staccato* (which is an Italian word that means *detached*). A *dot* placed above or below a note, generally at the note head side rather than the stem side, indicates that the note should be cut short, so that it is detached (noticeably separated) from the note that follows. By the way, previously we said that a *dot* lengthens the duration of a note by half the note's value. More technically, that type of dot is known as an *augmentation dot* (but it's usually called simply a *dot* as a kind of shorthand)— and that kind of dot is placed *after* (not above or below) the note. The dot that indicates *staccato* is called, not surprisingly, a *staccato dot,* but it too is often called simply a *dot* as a kind of shorthand.

Take a look at the example below, which is the opening melody of "Merrily We Roll Along." The dot on beat 4 of measure 1 and beats 2 and 4 of measure 2 shows that the note in question is cut short; in other words, it's performed more like an eighth note, followed by an eighth rest, than a quarter note.

Mer - ri - ly   we roll   a - long,   roll   a - long,   roll   a - long...

About legato: Successive notes are usually played fairly smoothly if there's no indication to the contrary, meaning that each note is held for its full value. However, to emphasize the fact that they're played smoothly, or to indicate that they're to be played especially smoothly, a *slur* can be used to connect them. A slur is a curved line connecting notes of different pitch; it indicates that the notes are to be connected in a smooth manner. (Remember: a curved line connecting notes of the *same* pitch is a *tie*, not a slur.) The example above uses a slur to show that the first four notes are smoothly connected. The technical term for a smooth connection of notes is *legato* (an Italian word that literally means *bound*). And, in fact, another way to indicate that notes are to be smoothly connected is to simply write the word *legato* beneath them (that is, *instead* of writing a slur).

Note: As stated previously, a slur in *vocal* music is used to show that two or more notes are sung on a single syllable, and those notes are automatically smoothly connected when you sing. But in instrumental music, and also sometimes in vocal music, a slur is used to show that a certain *phrase* is to be played smoothly. Think of the music above as an instrumental example; the lyrics are included only for reference—to help you find your place in the song.

In music written for the piano, another way to show that notes are smoothly connected is to indicate that you press down the *sustain pedal* (also called the *sustaining pedal* and the *damper pedal*) with your foot (you know, the pedal on the right, when you're seated at the piano). Holding down the sustain pedal not only connects the notes smoothly, but it also causes them to sustain, until the pedal is lifted. The abbreviation *Ped.* beneath the bass clef of the grand staff indicates that the sustain pedal should be depressed. And an asterisk (*) indicates that the pedal should be lifted. Another method of indicating that the sustain pedal should be depressed (and eventually lifted) is by means of horizontal brackets (with vertical jags at the beginning and end), encompassing the notes in question; these brackets are also placed beneath the grand staff. By the way, a pedal indication often occurs when the notes of a chord are written one at a time (as, say, consecutive 16th notes or eighth notes), but when the intention is that the notes ring out to form full-sounding chords.

About accent marks: An accent mark in music looks like this: >. It indicates that the note it appears above (or sometimes below) should be *accented*; that is, it should be played louder than normal in order to stress it. In the example above, you see this on the first note. Of course, technically, the first note of any measure automatically is more stressed than the other notes; but to emphasize the fact, or to make that note even more stressed than usual, an accent mark can be used. Note: If an accent mark points upward (∧) rather than to the right, it is said to be a *marcato* mark, and it indicates that the note in question is to be stressed even more, played even louder, than a note with a regular accent mark; in other words, it indicates that the note is *very* accented.

EXPRESSION

About dynamics: The word *dynamics* is a general term that denotes the varying levels of volume in music. You can have music that's played loudly, or that's played softly, or that's played loudly in some portions and softly in others—with the change from one to the other either sudden or gradual. Certain words and symbols in the music tell you how loudly or softly you should play.

Because historically Italian composers were influential in the musical world, verbal indications in music, whether full words or abbreviations, are generally written in Italian rather than English (as you saw with *staccato* and *legato,* discussed above). Various volume indications are also given in Italian, but they are almost always abbreviated. For example, the indication to play loudly is the Italian word *forte* (meaning *loud* or *loudly*), which is written in the musical score in bold, italic type as simply *f*. And the indication to play softly is the Italian word *piano*, meaning *soft* or *softly*, which is written in the musical score as simply *p*.

The list below gives the Italian words for a range of dynamic levels from extremely soft to extremely loud. Each level is preceded by its standard abbreviation, as seen in a musical score, and is followed by its translation into English.

ppp	*pianississimo,* extremely soft		*mf*	*mezzo forte,* moderately loud
pp	*pianissimo,* very soft		*f*	*forte,* loud
p	*piano,* soft		*ff*	*fortissimo,* very loud
mp	*mezzo piano,* moderately soft		*fff*	*fortississimo,* extrememely loud

A famous use of contrasting dynamics in a piece is Haydn's Symphony No. 94, the so-called *Surprise Symphony*. As seen in the excerpt below, Haydn begins with a dynamic level of *piano*. Because the music is mellow and played softly for a while, the audience becomes very relaxed. Then, a sudden very loud note (see last note of excerpt) startles them. That's the surprise, and the reason the symphony is so nicknamed.

The example above shows a *sudden* change of dynamic level. To show a *gradual* change from one level to another, special symbols, sometimes called *wedges,* or *hairpins* (because they resemble hairpins), are employed, as in the example below, in which it's indicated that the music becomes gradually louder (as the melody moves upward) and then gradually softer (as the melody moves back down). The technical terms for these indications (that is, the Italian terms) are *crescendo* (abbreviated *cresc.*) for a gradual *increase* in volume (hairpin opens to the right), and either *diminuendo* (abbreviated *dim.*) or *decrescendo* (abbreviated *decresc.*) for a gradual *decrease* in volume (hairpin closes to the right). In the example below, instead of drawing hairpins, the notator could have written *cresc.* after the first dynamic mark *(mp)* and either *dim.* or *decresc.* after the second *(mf)*. By the way, to emphasize the fact that a particular dynamic change is to be made suddenly rather than gradually, the notator can write the Italian word *subito* (meaning *immediately*), or its abbreviation, *sub.*, along with (usually just before) a new dynamic marking, as in *sub. ff*.

Note that whereas some aspects of music are very precise (for example, the tempo of a certain song might be exactly 120 beats per minute), dynamics are not precise; that is, there is no corresponding decibel level for each musical dynamic level. Instead the performer plays in a way that, to him, is *forte,* or *mezzo piano,* or whatever the case may be. Also note that in centuries past (for example, in Bach's time), composers generally didn't indicate dynamics, thus leaving it up the performer to decide how loudly or softly to play a piece.

About tempo: Probably the first thing you notice when looking at a piece of music is what's placed above the top line of music, all the way to the left—the so-called *tempo heading.* This is what tells you how fast or slowly to play the piece; the word *tempo* comes from the Italian word *tempus,* meaning *time.* You may know, based on the time signature, that, let's say, the quarter note gets one beat—but you don't know, unless you look at the tempo heading, how fast the beats go by (that is, how fast you should tap your foot or count beats in your mind).

Many modern publications, especially of popular music, have tempo headings in English, generally in bold Roman type, and these are pretty much self-explanatory. For example, you may see such headings as **Fast, Moderately fast, Moderately slow,** and **Slowly.** Sometimes a certain style of music is included as part of the tempo heading (such as **Moderate Reggae,** or **Fast Rock**). But even though these heading are self-explanatory, it's worth noting that the tempo heading always refers to the speed of *beats,* not of *notes.* So, a piece may have a slow beat (slow foot tapping), as indicated by the tempo heading, but within each beat you may have many small notes (as when, for example, you have eight 32nd notes in a single beat of 4/4 time). To state it again, what's important to remember is that the tempo heading tells you how fast the *beats* go by, not how fast *individual notes* go by.

While some publications have tempo headings in English, others (especially of classical music) have them in Italian (again in bold Roman type). Below is a list of common Italian tempo headings, from extremely slow to extremely fast; after each is its English translation.

Grave, extremely slow   **Moderato,** moderately

Largo, very slow   **Allegro,** fast

Adagio, slow   **Vivace,** very fast

Andante, moderately slow   **Presto,** extremely fast

If a composer wishes to modify the tempo *within* a piece, he uses Italian terms (or rather, abbreviations of these terms) to indicate this. For example, the abbreviation *rit.* (or sometimes *ritard.*) stands for *ritardando,* which means to slow down gradually. This indication is often found near a piece's ending. (Interestingly, performers sometimes take it upon themselves to slow down a bit at the very end of a piece even if *rit.* isn't indicated). Another word that means the same thing as *ritardando* (to slow down gradually) is *rallentando,* abbreviated *rall.* Conversely, to indicate a gradual *increase* in tempo, *accel.* (abbreviation of *accelerando*) is used. In addition to these terms, the Italian phrase *poco a poco* (meaning *little by little*), as in *rit. poco a poco,* can be added to show that a change is *very* gradual rather than merely gradual.

ABOUT FORM AND SIGNS OF REPETITION

When talking about popular music, the word *form* usually refers to how the various sections of a song are put together, especially in terms of how they repeat. For example, a song that consists of Verse, Chorus, Verse, Chorus is said to be—for obvious reasons—in ABAB form; and a song made up of Verse, Verse, Bridge, Verse is said to be in AABA form. In classical music, the individual movements of larger pieces (such as symphonies and concertos) are generally longer than popular songs, and so involve more complex forms, with such names as *sonata form, rondo form,* and *theme and variations form* (whose structures we needn't deal with here).

But for the purposes of this book, when we talk about form, we're really talking about various signs and symbols that indicate that certain measures, passages, or sections of a piece are to be repeated (that is, played two or more times rather than just once). The general purpose of *repeats* (sections that are repeated) is to save space on the printed page.

In the example that follows, the beginning of the Christmas carol "Angels We Have Heard on High," the symbols at the beginning and end are *repeat signs.* A repeat sign consists of a thick and a thin bar line, with two dots next to them; the dots straddle the middle staff line. The first repeat sign below is an *opening* repeat, and the one at the end is a *closing* repeat. The opening and closing repeat signs together indicate that the material between them (whether one measure, a few measures, or many measures) is to be repeated (played twice in a row). But note that even though part of a repeat sign looks like a bar line, the repeat sign itself is not actually a bar line; as such, a repeat sign is sometimes found *within* an individual measure. If you see two sets of lyrics under the notes of a repeated section, it's understood that you sing the top lyric the first time through and the bottom lyric the second time through. If you mentally sing through the example below, you see that in this famous carol the first four measures of the song are indeed sung twice, and that repeats signs can be used as a space saver.

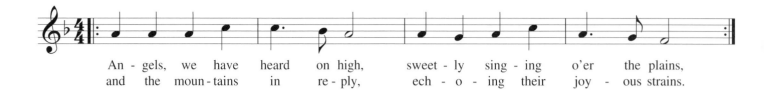

An - gels, we have heard on high, sweet - ly sing - ing o'er the plains,
and the moun - tains in re - ply, ech - o - ing their joy - ous strains.

Sometimes you have a repeated section that ends one way the first time through, but another way the second time through. This is achieved with so-called *ending brackets,* as illustrated in the example below. To state the obvious, on the first time through, play the measure or measures under the *first ending* bracket; the second time through, play the measure or measures under the *second ending* bracket, skipping over the measures under the first ending bracket. Your familiarity with the song of this example—the Christmas carol "God Rest Ye Merry, Gentlemen"—should make clear how ending brackets work. But to state how the example is played in terms of measure numbers: The first time through, after the pickup note, play measures 1, 2, 3, and 4; the second time through, play measures 1, 2, 3, and 5, and then continue to measure 6 and rest of the song.

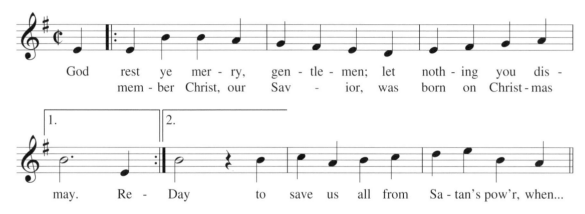

God rest ye mer - ry, gen - tle - men; let noth - ing you dis -
mem - ber Christ, our Sav - ior, was born on Christ - mas

1.   2.

may. Re - Day to save us all from Sa - tan's pow'r, when...

The next example, the beginning of the Christmas song "Carol of the Bells," features another kind of repeat sign (as seen in measures 2, 3, and 4). This sign, sometimes called a *simile mark* (from the Italian word *simile,* meaning *similar*) consists of a slanted line (usually extending from the second to the fourth staff line) with a dot on either side of it (with the dot to the left in the third space and the dot to the right in the second space). The sign signifies that you play, in the measure with the sign, exactly what you played in the previous measure. This type of repeat symbol isn't a space saver in terms of how many measures are written, but it can save space in terms of how wide a measure is (that is, you can have just that sign instead of, say, sixteen 16th notes).

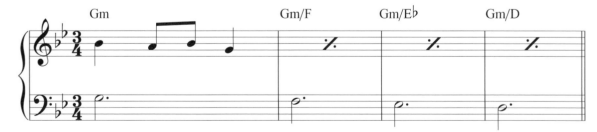

A point of interest: A musical phrase that's repeated often is known as a *motif,* or *motive.* Often, for the sake of variety, a motive will begin from a different note each time it's repeated. For example, think of the opening of Beethoven's Fifth Symphony: dah-dah-dah-DAAAH (and then from another pitch) dah-dah-dah-DAAAH. But if a motive keeps repeating from the *same* pitch (as in "Carol of the Bells"), something else is needed in the composition to provide interest (to prevent monotony). In the case of this song, it's the bass line, which moves stepwise—in dotted half notes—down the G minor scale. Note that we put this example on the grand staff and include the bass line. We do this to avoid the monotony of nothing but a short phrase repeated over and over, but we also do it to give you an opportunity to play piano music as it is generally written in actual practice—with both hands playing at the same time, in contrasting rhythms. In this case you play with both hands on the first beat of each measure, and then with just the right hand on beats 2 and 3, while the left hand note continues to ring.

Another point of interest: Sometimes in printed music you see letters above certain notes. In the example above, for example, you see Gm, Gm/F, and so on. These are *chord symbols*. (A *chord* is a group of notes sounding together, usually producing a pleasing sound, or harmony.) They're sometimes included so that if someone who plays an instrument capable of producing chords, such as guitar or piano, wishes to provide an accompaniment, he will know which chords to play. Taking the chord symbols in the example above: Gm stands for "G minor," meaning that the accompanist should play a G minor chord. (By the way, in order to simply read music, you don't need to know that the notes that make up a G minor chord happen to be G, B♭, and D, but most accompanists will know this.) Also, it's understood, from the chord name, that the bottommost note of the chord the accompaniment plays should be the note the chord is named after, the so-called *root* of the chord—in this case, G; and if a bass player joins in the accompaniment, the Gm chord symbol tells him to play that bottommost note, G, on his bass. But if a note other than the root is desired as the bass note (as the bottommost note), the desired bass pitch is written after the chord name, with a slash mark separating the two. So, Gm/F (pronounced "G minor over F") means to play a G minor chord, but with an F in the bass.

A technical point: We mentioned that the repeat symbol described above is sometimes called a *simile mark*. But the word *simile* itself (or, more commonly, its abbreviation, *sim.),* is used in music notation to show that a certain notation (a particular articulation, for example) that has been indicated should continue (in a similar fashion). For example, let's say that in the song "Carol of the Bells" we want all the melody notes to be played staccato. We can include a staccato dot on each note throughout the song, *or* we can write staccato dots for just one or two measures and then indicate *sim.* (or *simile*) above the following measure, indicating that the staccato articulation should continue. By the way, to indicate that a particular notation should continue not only in a similar fashion for some length of time but *always and throughout* the piece, the word *sempre* (an Italian word meaning *always*) is used instead of *simile*. So, if you see the word *sempre* after, say, two measures of staccato, you know that the notes will *always* be staccato *throughout* the whole piece, saving you the trouble of looking out for if and when the staccato articulations might happen to end.

Sometimes, again to save space (or to save whole pages of music), notators indicate that a certain section of music is to be played again, but not immediately after it was just played. For example, let's say a piece is in ABA form, with each section consisting of 16 measures. Instead of seeing all 48 measures written out, you're likely to see just the first 32 measures (the AB portion), and then a verbal instruction (in Italian) telling you to repeat the A section. This is accomplished by means of the phrase *D.C. al Fine,* in which *D.C.* stands for *Da capo* (meaning "from the top," or, literally, "from the head"), and *Fine* (pronounced *FEE-nay*) means *end*—but not the actual end of the score, but a place within the score marked as an end (after an earlier section has recurred) by means of the word *Fine* placed above a particular note or rest, or at the end of a particular phrase or measure. So, *D.C. al Fine* indicates that you go back to the beginning of the piece and play until the spot marked *Fine*. The example that follows, the well-know French children's song "Au clair de la lune," shows a *D.C. al Fine* in action. Note that the first instance of the A section contains a repeat. If you're familiar with the song, you know that the recurrence of the A section doesn't include one. An instruction as to whether to include repeats on a *D.C.* usually appears parenthetically beneath the *D.C.* indication, as seen at the end of the example.

Sometimes a section that *doesn't* start at the very beginning of the piece is to be repeated, and sometimes the ending of that section is *different* from how it is played the first time. In such a case, the Italian instruction *D.S. al Coda* is used, in which *D.S.* stand for *Dal segno* (pronounced *SAY-nyo*) and means "from the sign," and *Coda* signifies a special ending marked with a so-called *coda sign* (and usually the word *Coda,* as well). The example below, the Christmas carol "O Christmas Tree" displays a *D.S. al Coda* in action. The *segno* (sign) looks kind of like a capital *S* with a slash through it and two dots around it. This is seen in the example below above the opening repeat sign of measure 1. The coda sign looks like a circle, or a capital *O,* with a vertical and a horizontal line through it. This is seen at measure 10 below. So, *D.S. al Coda* means to go back to the sign, then play through the measure marked *To Coda,* then skip to the special ending section marked *Coda* and play that. Your familiarity with "O Christmas Tree" should make the structure below, and the meaning of *D.S. al Coda,* clear. But to spell out the structure (with both its *repeats* and its *D.S. al Coda*) in measure numbers, you play (after the opening pickup) measures 1, 2, 3, 4, then 1, 2, 3, 5, 6, 7, 8, 9, then 1, 2, 3, 10.

Note that a *D.C.* can be used with either a *Fine* or a *Coda,* and that as *D.S.* also can be used with either a *Fine* or a *Coda.* So in addition to *D.C. al Fine* and *D.S. al Coda,* you might see *D.C. al Coda* (from the beginning, then skipping at a certain point to the Coda) and *D.S. al Fine* (from the sign until the spot marked *Fine*).

ABOUT ORNAMENTS

In music, and also generally speaking, an ornament is a decorative embellishment. If you listen to the beginning of Bach harpsichord piece known as the *Goldberg Variations,* you'll hear all kinds of ornaments being played. Back in Bach's time's, the Baroque era (16th and early 17th centuries), ornaments were extremely common. In fact, the word *baroque* means *ornate.* Today, fewer types of ornaments are used, but two of them are especially worthy of note: the *grace note* and the *trill.*

About the grace note: A *grace note* is a small-sized note, perhaps half or two-thirds the size of a regular note, usually with a slash through its stem. It's placed just before a normal note, and usually slurred to it. The grace note has no time value of its own; instead, it "steals" a bit of time from the main note that follows it. Think of a drum quickly going *ka-BOOM*. The *ka* is the sound of the grace note and the *BOOM* is the sound of the regular note. The example below, Beethoven's famous "Turkish March," gives you a chance to see and to play grace notes. Remember: Don't count out the grace notes; rather, on beat 1 of measures 1 and 2, think of the G-sharp and the A practically as a single unit (like the drum's *ka-BOOM*) occurring on the downbeat.

Note that even though the example above features single grace notes, double grace notes (beamed together as small 16th notes, and sounding like *ka-ka-BOOM*), triple grace notes (three small 16th notes sounding like *ka-ka-ka-BOOM*) notes, and even quadruple grace notes also occur.

About the trill: A rapid alternation between two notes that are a half step or a whole step apart is known as a *trill* (as when you play, say, A then B then A then B and so on, back and forth, very quickly). The exact speed of the alternation is at the discretion of the performer. It might be slightly rapid, moderately rapid, very rapid, or as rapid as possible. The example below is the final four measures of the Christmas carol "O Come, All Ye Faithful" ("O come let us adore Him, Christ the Lord") played three times in succession (notated here with the help of repeats and 1st, 2nd, and 3rd endings). In the 1st ending, the music is written how the song is normally played. In the second ending, the dotted quarter note A is replaced with a decorative flourish in the form of mostly 16th notes alternating between A and B. This is a trill that's shown with actual note values. In the 3rd ending, the trill is indicated as it would be in actual practice; that is, as a bold, italic **tr** with a horizontal wavy line after it, extending as far as the trill should last. When a trill is notated this way, the performer, as stated, decides exactly how fast to alternate between the written note and the note a step above it, probably faster than in the 16th-note version shown in the 2nd ending.

Note that the trill above involves notes a whole step apart. The general rule for playing a trill is to alternate between the notated pitch and the tone a step above that's *in the key you're in.* Because the key of G contains a B♮, A alternates with B (not with B♭). But if you were to play a trill on a B, you would alternate with C, a *half step* above (because C is the step, or scale degree, above B in the key of G). If, hypothetically, a notator writing in the key of G *does* want to indicate a trill between A and B♭, he still writes an A note, but places a small flat sign to the right of, or above, the **tr** that's placed above the A. Also note that while most trills contain a wavy line, trills on short notes (one beat or less) usually do not (that is, they are indicated with only a **tr** above the note in question).

About tremolo: Whereas a trill is a rapid alternation between two pitches a step apart, a tremolo is a rapid alternation between two pitches *more* than a step apart. It produces a "trembling" sound. By the way, a tremolo is usually not classified as an ornament per se, because it doesn't "decorate" a particular note; but we include it here owing to its similarity to the trill. Note that as with a trill, the speed of alternation between the notes of a tremolo is at the discretion of the performer—but, generally speaking, the alternation in a tremolo is as fast as possible.

A tremolo can be notated in one of two ways, each of which generally involves what look like three slanted beams, all or some of which are rather short. The three beams represent, or at least give the impression of, 32nd notes, which are obviously very quick notes—though technically, tremolos are not actually played as 32nds; they're simply played very quickly. The example below shows both methods of notation. In measures 1 and 2, the slanted beams are placed *above* the note heads. In measures 3 and 4, which are identical to measures 1 and 2, but notated differently, the beams are placed *between* the note heads. The second method, placing beams between note heads, is more common. To play a tremolo, simply alternate between the notes shown as rapidly as possible; for example, to play measure 1, alternate between C and E for the duration of four beats.

Note in measures 1 and 2 above that when there is no stem, the slanted beams go above the note heads, but that if there is a stem, the beams go *through* the stem. Also note that in beat 4 of measure 2, only *two* beams go through the stem; that's because the eighth note beam itself is counted as one of the (total of three) beams. Likewise, a 16th note, with two real beams (or flags) of its own, would require only *one* slanted tremolo beam.

In the second half of the example above (measures 3 and 4), it's a bit easier to see that you're alternating between two separate pitches. However, this notation method requires the notator to write what looks like twice as many beats as necessary in each measure; for example, measure 3 has *two* whole notes instead of just one. When you read this type of tremolo notation, be aware that *each* of the two pitches involved is shown for its full rhythmic value, and mentally make the proper adjustment, by counting beats for just one of the two notes rather than both.

Tremolos can involve not only individual notes, but chords as well. Imagine that in measure 3 above you see a whole-note G sitting directly above the whole-note E. That would tell you to alternate between middle C (played, let's say, on piano with your right-hand thumb) and E and G struck together (played on piano with your right-hand index and ring fingers), producing a trembling chord (in this case, a C major chord). By the way, a very rapid (generally as fast as possible) reiteration of the *same* pitch—as when a mandolin player very rapidly restrikes a long note, or when a drummer plays a roll—is also called a tremolo.

About arpeggiated chords: Another technique that's not an ornament per se but that's ornamental in effect is the *arpeggio* (or the *arpeggiated chord*). An arpeggio is a chord played *one note at a time,* in succession. Often the notes of an arpeggio are written in a particular rhythm, such as steady eighth notes or 16th notes. But if a composer wishes to indicate that a chord be simply rolled from bottom to top in a rapid manner, without giving the individual notes of the chord time values of their own, he indicates this by placing a wavy vertical line to the left of the chord in question. You've probably heard this effect played on a harp.

In the example below, the first measure shows an arpeggio of a C major chord notated in time, as 16th notes; note that here, once a note has been struck, it is then tied to the following notes to show that it isn't restruck but that it continues to ring. Measure 2 is similar in effect to measure 1, but here the performer rolls the chord not in actual 16th notes, but simply rapidly, at a speed of his whim; in reading the music, he thinks of all of the arpeggiated chord as being struck on beat 1. If a notator wishes to indicate that an arpeggiated chord is rolled *downward,* from top to bottom, he simply places a downward-pointed arrowhead at the bottom of the wavy line.

ADDITIONAL SIGNS AND SYMBOLS

Certain musical symbols don't fall neatly into any particular category. In this section we look at a few more noteworthy symbols concerning pitch and rhythm.

Symbols concerning pitch: In Chapter 4 you learned that the black keys on the piano are indicated by means of sharps and flats, and that the white keys are known as "natural notes." But white keys, in certain situations, can also be indicated with sharps and flats. You understand that adding a sharp to a note raises that note by one key on the piano (and adding a flat to a note lowers that note by one key on the piano), and you understand that there is no black key on the piano between E and F and between B and C. Consequently, an E♯ note is the same key on the piano as F♮; and a C♭ note is the same key on the piano as B♮.

Sometimes, due to theoretical considerations, a note (letter name) may need to be *doubly* sharped (raised two keys on the piano), or *doubly* flatted (lowered two keys on the piano). And so you sometimes hear such terms as "F-double-sharp" and "B-double-flat." The example below illustrates the use of a *double sharp* in the song "Greensleeves" (also known as "What Child Is This?"), here in the key of G♯ minor. The double sharp symbol itself looks kind of like an *x* (see measures 3 and 4 below). It indicates to play the natural note in question *two* piano keys higher. Here, the double sharp is on F, so you play it on the G♮ key, a white key two piano keys above F.

You may wonder why F✗ is used above instead of G♮. The answer is that the melody is based on a scale—here the G♯ minor scale, as indicated by the G♯ minor key signature. And major and minor scales, as you know, are made up of consecutive letters, with none skipped or repeated. So, the seventh degree of a G♯ minor scale must be some kind of F. Since this song employs the version of the minor scale known as *harmonic minor,* the seventh degree (as you remember from Chapter 4) is raised a half step compared to how it appears in the natural minor scale. Raising F♯ a half step, but keeping the F letter name, yields F✗.

A *double flat* lowers a note (letter name) by two piano keys. So, for example, B-double-flat is played on the A♮ white key. The double-flat symbol itself is two flat symbols side by side, with no space between. Again, due to such considerations as scales and harmony, a double flat, rather than a natural note, is sometimes required. In the example below, an excerpt from Chopin's famous "Minute Waltz," in the key of D♭ major, you see the double flat in action (measure 6).

You know that to indicate that a certain passage is to be played an octave higher than written, the symbol *8va* (with a dashed line after it) is placed above the notes in question. But sometimes notes go so incredibly high that even with the use of an *8va* sign there are still more ledger lines above the staff than desired. In such a case, the notator can use a symbol to show that a note or passage is played *two* octaves higher than written. You might think the symbol for this indication would be *16va,* but it is actually *15ma.* (If you count white piano keys from C to another C two octaves higher, you see that there are 15 keys, not 16—because the C in the middle is counted only once, not twice). The symbol *15ma* stands for the Italian word *quindicesima,* meaning *at the 15th,* which means *at the double octave* (meaning, *play two octaves higher than written*). You might see the *15ma* symbol when, for example, a note or chord is played several times, with each successive time an octave higher than the previous one. The example below shows how such a situation might look both *without* the use of the *8va* and *15ma* symbols (measure 1, with an uncomfortably large number of ledger lines) and *with* the symbols (measure 2).

Symbols concerning rhythm: You know that silences are indicated with rests, and for each note value there is a corresponding rest. But sometimes in written music you see a symbol for a pause, which is like a rest, but it's not counted in actual time as a rest is; instead, the length of the pause is at the whim of the performer, but it's generally brief.

A short pause is indicated by a bold comma placed above the staff at the appropriate moment, as seen in measure 2 below. This symbol can be called a *breath mark* or a *comma*. Although it often occurs in vocal music, sometimes literally signifying that the singer should take a breath, it also appears in instrumental music. In each case it signifies a slight pause. This becomes clear if you think of singing, as shown below: "…o'er the land of the free (pause) and the home of the brave."

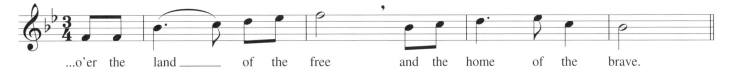

The example below, the bugle call "Taps," illustrates two additional symbols that affect rhythm but are not counted in actual time; rather, their durations are again at the whim of the performer. A *caesura*, indicated by two slanted lines going through the top staff line (see measures 1 and 2 below), is like a comma (breath mark), but it's actually more pronounced, or even longer. It's a very deliberate pause or break (a silence) between phrases. You might hear such a pause between the end of a hymn and a final "Amen."

The symbol below that looks like the top half of a circle with a dot under it (see measures 1, 2, and 4) is a *fermata* (or, as some people refer to it, a *bird's eye*). It indicates that the note below is to be held longer than normal. The exact length is, as stated, at the whim of the performer, but, though it's longer than normal, it's usually not overly long; otherwise, a longer note value, or several tied notes, would have been indicated instead. If you're playing in an ensemble with a conductor, the conductor will indicate how long the note in question should be held, by showing its cut-off with a hand gesture. Look at the music below and imagine playing it. How long would you hold each note with a fermata above it? And how long of a break would you allow for each caesura?

CHAPTER 8
THREE CLASSICS FOR YOU TO PLAY

In this chapter you get to reward yourself for all your hard work—and you get a chance to apply your knowledge of reading music—by playing an excerpt (the first several measures) from a keyboard piece by each of the world's three greatest composers of all time: Johann Sebastian Bach, Wolfgang Amadeus Mozart, and Ludwig van Beethoven. Each piece is one that pianists love to play, and you've probably heard each of them at some time or another.

BACH

First is Bach's "Prelude in C" from *The Well-Tempered Clavier*, which consists of nothing but arpeggiated chords in a steady 16th-note rhythm, with the second half of each measure the same as the first. Note that in the left-hand part, the half notes have stems pointing downward and the dotted eighths tied to quarters have stems pointing up. Just as the right hand and left hand can play contrasting rhythms on the piano, so can the individual fingers of a single hand. So, for the left-hand part, first use one finger to strike the half note, and hold the note for two beats by keeping the finger pressed down, then (after a 16th rest) use another finger to strike the upstem note, holding that down along with the already-sounding half note. Note that Bach wrote this piece for the harpsichord, which doesn't have a sustain pedal; that perhaps explains why Bach wrote the left-hand part as sustained notes, rather than as simply 16th notes with a *Ped.* indication for every two beats.

By the way, the famous song "Ave Maria," which is often heard at weddings and funerals (but not the *other* famous "Ave Maria," by Franz Schubert) consists of an accompaniment that is Bach's "Prelude in C" and a melody, superimposed over that accompaniment, composed—more than 130 years after Bach wrote his "Prelude"—by French composer Charles Gounod. Because Bach's piece is nothing but chords, with no melody of its own, it's not surprising that someone—in this case, Gounod, best known as the composer of "Funeral March of a Marionette" and of the opera *Faust*—would come along and add a melody.

Bach didn't indicate any tempo or dynamics for this piece (most composers of his era, the Baroque era, didn't), so play it at a speed and volume level that feels comfortable to you.

MOZART

The next piece is the beginning of Mozart's Piano Sonata No. 16 in C major. You may be familiar with the 1963 Top 20 pop hit "Somewhere," by the Tymes, which is based on it. The left-hand part provides an accompaniment, notated by Mozart in treble clef because the notes are rather high and would require excessive ledger lines if bass clef were used, and the right-hand part is the melody. Note that the accompaniment consists of arpeggiated chords (here in steady eighth notes), and that the order of successive notes, for each chord, is *lowest, highest, middle, highest*. This particular pattern of arpeggiation, because it was employed extensively by Italian composer Domenico Alberti, has come to be known as an *Alberti bass*. Many composers of Mozart's era, the Classical era, made use of it.

Measure 4 gives you a chance to play a short trill (between the notated pitch, F, and the G a step above). Because the trilled note is so short (half a beat only), no wavy line is necessary after the *tr*.

Although Mozart indicated a tempo for this piece, he offered no dynamic level; so the volume level is up to you. Although a fast tempo is indicated, start practicing the piece slowly, perhaps practicing each hand's part individually at first. With some practice you should be able to play it at the tempo indicated, *allegro*.

BEETHOVEN

The final piece is the beginning of Beethoven's famous "Moonlight Sonata" (officially called Piano Sonata No. 14 in C-sharp Minor, First Movement). In the two pieces above you played arpeggiated chords with four notes to the beat—as steady 16th notes (Bach), and then with two notes to the beats—as steady eighth notes (Mozart). Here you play arpeggiated chords with three notes to the beat—as steady eighth-note triplets.

Note that an italic numeral *3* appears above only the first two triplets. The *sim.* (short for *simile*) indication on beat 3 tells you to continue in similar manner; in other words, continue playing the three-note groupings as triplets.

The left-hand part is written in octaves, so you'll have to stretch your left hand a bit, using thumb and pinky, to play both notes at the same time.

Beethoven indicated both tempo and dynamics for this piece. The *pp* tells you to play *pianissimo* (very soft). The *adagio* portion of the tempo heading tells you to play slowly (that is, the beats themselves—not the individual notes that make up each triplet—go by slowly). The *sostenuto* portion of the tempo heading is an instruction to allow the notes to sustain beyond their normal values; in other words, for each beat, the first note of the triplet should be held throughout the beat (like a quarter note), and the second note should also be held through the end of the beat (forming a full sounding chord on each beat rather than three short individual notes). You can achieve this effect either by holding down the keys with your right hand till the end of each beat, or you can use the sustain pedal with you foot, lifting it and repressing each time the chord changes.

You may wonder why Beethoven wrote this piece in simple time (rather than compound time, such as 12/8) if all the beats are divided into thirds. The answer is that the *melody* of the piece (which enters immediately after the introduction presented here and which is played mainly by the right-hand pinky) contains figures, such as a dotted eighth followed by a 16th, that are typical of simple time.

Interestingly, Beethoven wrote this piece with a signature of cut time (equivalent to 2/2 time, not 4/4 time)—meaning that every *six* right hand notes (not every three notes) is one slow beat. However, today, nearly all pianists perform the piece as if written in 4/4 time, and that's how we've presented it here.

Final thoughts: By now, if you've worked your way steadily through this book, you should have a pretty good idea of how to read music—even though you played all the examples only on the piano and on no other instrument. But the good news is that all the basic concepts of reading music apply to any instrument you might want to learn, whether it's a guitar or a flute or a violin. Of course, to play another instrument, you'll need to learn how to finger it (with the help of a teacher, or perhaps simply by means of a fingering chart). But much of the hard work—understanding the ins and outs of music notation—you've already accomplished.

ABOUT THE AUTHOR

Mark Phillips is an author, guitarist, arranger, editor, and publisher with more than 40 years in the music publishing field. He earned his bachelor's degree in music theory from Case Western Reserve University and his master's degree from Northwestern University. While working toward a doctorate in music theory at Northwestern, Phillips taught classes in theory, ear-training, sight-singing, counterpoint, and guitar.

During the 1970s and early '80s, Phillips was Director of Popular Music at Warner Bros. Publications, where he edited and arranged the songbooks of such artists as Neil Young, James Taylor, the Eagles, and Led Zeppelin. From 1985 to 2013 he was Director of Music and Director of Publications at Cherry Lane Music, where he edited or arranged the songbooks of such artists as John Denver, Van Halen, Guns N' Roses, and Metallica, and served as Music Editor of the magazines *Guitar* and *Guitar One*.

Phillips is the author of several books on musical subjects, including *Guitar for Dummies*, *Metallica Riff by Riff*, *Sight-Sing Any Melody Instantly*, and *Sight-Read Any Rhythm Instantly*. In his non-musical life, Phillips is the author/publisher of a series of "fun" high school textbooks, including *The Wizard of Oz Vocabulary Builder*, *The Pinocchio Intermediate Vocabulary Builder*, *Tarzan and Jane's Guide to Grammar*, and *Conversations in Early American History: 1492–1837*.

Great Harmony & Theory Helpers

HAL LEONARD HARMONY & THEORY
by George Heussenstamm
Hal Leonard

These books are designed for anyone wishing to expand their knowledge of music theory, whether beginner or more advanced. The first two chapters deal with music fundamentals, and may be skipped by those with music reading experience.
00312062 Part 1 – Diatonic $27.50
00312064 Part 2 – Chromatic $27.50

BERKLEE MUSIC THEORY BOOK 1 – 2ND EDITION
by Paul Schmeling
Berklee Press

This essential method features rigorous, hands-on, "ears-on" practice exercises that help you explore the inner working of music, presenting notes, scales, and rhythms as they are heard in pop, jazz, and blues. You will learn and build upon the basic concepts of music theory with written exercises, listening examples, and ear training exercises.
50449615...$24.99

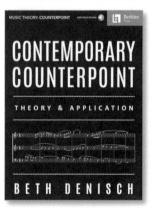

CONTEMPORARY COUNTERPOINT
Theory & Application
by Beth Denisch
Berklee Press

Use counterpoint to make your music more engaging and creative. Counterpoint – the relationship between musical voices – is among the core principles for writing music, and it has been central to the study of composition for many centuries. Whether you are a composer, arranger, film composer, orchestrator, music director, bandleader, or improvising musician, this book will help hone your craft, gain control, and lead you to new creative possibilities.
00147050...$22.99

THE CHORD WHEEL
The Ultimate Tool for All Musicians
by Jim Fleser
Hal Leonard

Master chord theory ... in minutes! *The Chord Wheel* is a revolutionary device that puts the most essential and practical applications of chord theory into your hands. This tool will help you: Improvise and Solo – Talk about chops! Comprehend key structure like never before; Transpose Keys – Instantly transpose any progression into each and every key; Compose Your Own Music – Watch your songwriting blossom! No music reading is necessary.
00695579...$15.99

ENCYCLOPEDIA OF READING RHYTHMS
Text and Workbook for All Instruments
by Gary Hess
Musicians Institute Press

A comprehensive guide to notes, rests, counting, subdividing, time signatures, triplets, ties, dotted notes and rests, cut time, compound time, swing, shuffle, rhythm studies, counting systems, road maps and more!
00695145..$29.99

HARMONY AND THEORY
A Comprehensive Source for All Musicians
by Keith Wyatt and Carl Schroeder
Musicians Institute Press

This book is a step-by-step guide to MI's well-known Harmony and Theory class. It includes complete lessons and analysis of: intervals, rhythms, scales, chords, key signatures; transposition, chord inversions, key centers; harmonizing the major and minor scales; and more!
00695161..$22.99

MUSIC THEORY WORKBOOK
For All Musicians
by Chris Bowman
Hal Leonard

A self-study course with illustrations and examples for you to write and check your answers. Topics include: major and minor scales; modes and other scales; harmony; intervals; chord structure; chord progressions and substitutions; and more.
00101379..$12.99

JAZZOLOGY
The Encyclopedia of Jazz Theory for All Musicians
by Robert Rawlins and Nor Eddine Bahha
Hal Leonard

A one-of-a-kind book encompassing a wide scope of jazz topics, for beginners and pros of any instrument. A three-pronged approach was envisioned with the creation of this comprehensive resource: as an encyclopedia for ready reference, as a thorough methodology for the student, and as a workbook for the classroom, complete with ample exercises and conceptual discussion.
00311167..$19.99